HOW TO
Differentiate Instruction
IN Mixed-Ability
Classrooms

2ND EDITION

Carol Ann Tomlinson

Association for Supervision and Curriculum Development

Alexandria, Virginia USA

Association for Supervision and Curriculum Development
1703 N. Beauregard St. • Alexandria, VA 22311-1714 USA
Telephone: 1-800-933-2723 or 703-578-9600 • Fax: 703-575-5400
Web site: http://www.ascd.org • E-mail: member@ascd.org
Author guidelines: www.ascd.org/write

Printed in the United States of America.

ISBN-13: 978-0-87120-512-4   ISBN-10: 0-87120-512-2

ASCD Product No. 101043   s4/2001

Also available as an e-book through ebrary, netLibrary, and many online booksellers (see Books in Print for the ISBNs).

Library of Congress Cataloging-in-Publication Data

Tomlinson, Carol A.
  How to differentiate instruction in mixed-ability classrooms / Carol
Ann Tomlinson.— 2nd ed.
      p. cm.
Includes bibliographical references and index.
"ASCD product no. 101043"—T.p. verso.
  ISBN 0-87120-512-2 (alk. paper)
  1. Mixed ability grouping in education—United States. 2. Learning
ability. 3. Classroom management—United States. I. Title.
  LB3061.3 .T65 2001
  371.2'52—dc21
                                                    2001000344

10 09 08 07 06   12 11 10 9 8

How to Differentiate Instruction in Mixed-Ability Classrooms
2nd Edition

Foreword to the 2nd Edition

I am often asked these days why I think there is such a great interest in the topic of differentiating instruction. My best guess is that the interest is sparked by the realization that it's no longer possible to look at a group of students in a classroom and pretend they are essentially alike.

Even in the few years since the first edition of this book, academic diversity has increased in schools. Greater and greater numbers of second-language students take seats among students whose first language is English. Even the second-language learners vary greatly as a group—not only in their native tongues but also in their degree of experience with their native language and the sort of home support system that follows them to school.

Greater numbers of students are being diagnosed with attention-deficit and related disorders. Diagnosis of learning disability affects students in virtually all classrooms. In addition, students come to classrooms with highly advanced skills and understandings. They come with an array of physical handicaps. They represent cultures that vary in significant ways. Many students bring with them to school stresses from home that are too great for young shoulders to carry. Many students, of course, represent several of these realities—a very bright student whose learning disability masks his promise, a second-language learner whose family teeters on the edge of economic viability, and so on.

If we elect to use what we know about learning, and, in fact, about ourselves, as we craft classrooms, we acknowledge that students learn in varied ways—some by hearing, others by doing, some alone, others in the company of peers, some in a rapid-fire fashion, others reflectively. We acknowledge, too, that individuals are intrigued or even inspired by different topics or issues, and that curiosity and inspiration are powerful catalysts for learning. To teach well is to attend to all these things.

Differentiation suggests it is feasible to develop classrooms where realities of student variance can be addressed along with curricular realities. The idea is compelling. It challenges us to draw on our best knowledge of teaching and learning. It suggests that there is room for both equity and excellence in our classrooms.

As "right" as the approach we call differentiation seems, it promises no slick and ready solutions. Like most worthy ideas, it is complex. It calls on us to question, change, reflect, and change some more.

This second edition of *How to Differentiate Instruction in Mixed-Ability Classrooms* follows this evolutionary route. In the years since the first edition, I have had the benefit of probing questions and practical examples from many educators. This revision reflects an extension and refinement of the elements presented in the earlier version of the book, based in no small measure on dialogue with other educators.

I am grateful to ASCD for the opportunity to share reflections and insights fueled by many educators who work daily to ensure a good academic fit for each student who enters their classrooms. These teachers wrestle with standards-driven curriculum, grapple with a predictable shortage of time in the school day, and do battle with management issues in a busy classroom. These educators also derive energy from the challenge and insight from their students. I continue to be the beneficiary of their frontline work. I hope this small volume represents them well. I hope also that it clarifies and extends what I believe to be an essential discussion on how we can attain the ideal of a high-quality public education that exists to maximize the capacity of each learner who trusts us to direct the course of his or her learning.

Introduction

The students populating U.S. classrooms today are a diverse lot. They come from differing cultures and have different learning styles. They arrive at school with differing levels of emotional and social maturity. Their interests differ greatly, both in topic and intensity. At any given time, they reflect differing levels of academic readiness in various subjects—and in various facets of a single subject. And to complicate things even further, readiness and interest can vary for a given student over time and depending on the subject matter.

Teachers in mixed-ability classrooms face multiple challenges, at every grade level. Each September, many 1st graders arrive already able to read 3rd grade books with comprehension, while their peers grapple for months with the idea of left-to-right print progression or the difference between short and long vowels. Some 3rd graders make an independent leap from multiplication to division before any explanation has been offered. Many of these same children, when they reach middle school, also make connections between themes in social studies and literature, or apply advanced mathematical tools to solving science problems before other students in their classes grasp the main idea of a chapter in the textbook. In high school, students who may have been previously identified as "slow" or "average" may surprise everyone when they're able to develop a complex and articulate defense of a position related to scientific ethics or economic strategy. And some of their classmates who had, until now, found school a "cinch" must work hard to feel comfortable with applications at a more abstract level.

In life, kids can choose from a variety of clothing to fit their differing sizes, styles, and preferences. We understand, without explanation, that this makes them more comfortable and gives expression to their developing personalities. In school, modifying or differentiating instruction for students of differing readiness and interests is also more comfortable, engaging, and inviting. One-size-fits-all instruction will inevitably sag or pinch—exactly as single-size clothing would—students who differ in need, even if they are chronologically the same age.

Acknowledging that students learn at different speeds and that they differ widely in their ability to think abstractly or understand complex ideas is like acknowledging that students at any given age aren't all the same height: It is not a statement of worth, but of reality. To accommodate this reality, teachers can create a "user-friendly" environment, one in which they flexibly adapt pacing, approaches to learning, and channels for expressing learning in response to their students' differing needs.

While the goal for each student is challenge and substantial growth, teachers must often define *challenge and growth* differently in response to students' varying interests and readiness levels.

This book provides guidance for teachers who are interested in creating learning environments that address the diversity typical of mixed-ability classrooms. The principles and strategies included here can help teachers address a variety of learning profiles, interests, and readiness levels. The goal here is to help teachers determine what differentiated instruction is, why it is appropriate for all learners, how to begin to plan for it, and how to become comfortable enough with student differences to make school comfortable for each learner who comes their way.

WHAT Differentiated Instruction **IS—AND ISN'T**

Kids of the same age aren't all alike when it comes to learning, any more than they are alike in terms of size, hobbies, personality, or likes and dislikes. Kids do have many things in common because they are human beings and because they are all children, but they also have important differences. What we share in common makes us human. How we differ makes us individuals. In a classroom with little or no differentiated instruction, only student similarities seem to take center stage. In a differentiated classroom, commonalities are acknowledged and built upon, and student differences become important elements in teaching and learning as well.

At its most basic level, differentiating instruction means "shaking up" what goes on in the classroom so that students have multiple options for taking in information, making sense of ideas, and expressing what they learn. In other words, a differentiated classroom provides different avenues to acquiring content, to processing or making sense of ideas, and to developing products so that each student can learn effectively.

In many classrooms, the approach to teaching and learning is more unitary than differentiated. For example, 1st graders may listen to a story and then draw a picture about what they learned. While they may choose to draw different facets of the story, they all experienced the same content, and they all had the same sense-making or processing activity. A kindergarten class may have four centers that all students visit to complete the same activities in a week's time. Fifth graders may all listen to the same explanation about fractions and complete the same homework assignment. Middle school or high school students may sit through a lecture and a video to help them understand a topic in science or history. They will all read the same chapter, take the same notes, complete the same lab or end-of-chapter questions, and take the same quiz. Such classrooms are familiar, typical, and largely undifferentiated.

Most teachers (as well as students and parents) have clear mental images of such classrooms. After experiencing undifferentiated instruction over many years, it is often difficult to imagine what a differentiated classroom would look and feel like. How, educators wonder, can we make the shift from "single-size instruction" to differentiated instruction so we can better meet our students' diverse needs? Answering this question first requires clearing away some misperceptions.

What Differentiated Instruction Is NOT

Differentiated instruction is NOT the "Individualized Instruction" of the 1970s.

We were probably onto something important in the '70s when we experimented with what we then called individualized instruction. At least we understood that students have different learning profiles and that there is merit in meeting students where they are and helping them move on from there. One flaw in the '70s approach was that we tried doing something different for each of the 30-plus students in a single classroom. When each student had a different reading assignment, for example, it didn't take long for teachers to become exhausted. A second flaw was that in order to "match" each student's precise entry level, we chopped up instruction into skill fragments, thereby making learning fragmented and largely irrelevant.

While it is true that differentiated instruction offers several avenues to learning, it does not assume a separate level for each learner. It also focuses on meaningful learning or powerful ideas for all students. Differentiation is probably more reminiscent of the one-room-schoolhouse than of individualization. That model of

instruction recognized that the teacher needed to work sometimes with the whole class, sometimes with small groups, and sometimes with individuals. These variations were important in order both to move each student along in his particular understandings and skills as well as to build a sense of community in the group.

Differentiated instruction is NOT chaotic.

Most teachers remember the recurrent nightmare (and periodic reality) from their first year of teaching: losing control of student behavior. A benchmark of teacher development is the point at which the teacher has become secure and comfortable with classroom management. Fear of losing control of student behavior is a major obstacle for many teachers in establishing a flexible classroom. Teachers who differentiate instruction quickly point out that, if anything, they exert more leadership in their classrooms, not less.

Compared with teachers who offer a single approach to learning, teachers who differentiate instruction have to manage and monitor many activities simultaneously. And they still must help students in developing ground rules for behavior, give and monitor specific directions for activities, and direct the sequence of events in each learning experience. Effective differentiated classrooms include purposeful student movement and some purposeful student talking. They are not disorderly or undisciplined.

Differentiated instruction is NOT just another way to provide homogeneous grouping.

Our memories of undifferentiated classrooms probably include the bluebird, cardinal, and buzzard reading groups. Typically, a buzzard remained a buzzard, and a cardinal was forever a cardinal. Under this system, buzzards nearly always worked with buzzards on skills-focused tasks, while work done by cardinals was typically at "higher levels" of thought. In addition to being predictable, student assignment to groups was virtually always teacher-selected.

A hallmark of an effective differentiated classroom, by contrast, is the use of flexible grouping, which accommodates students who are strong in some areas and weaker in others. For example, a student may be great at interpreting literature, but not so strong in spelling, or great with map skills and not as quick at grasping patterns in history, or quick with math word problems but careless with computation. The teacher who uses flexible grouping also understands that some students may begin a new task slowly, and then launch ahead at remarkable speed, while others will learn, but more slowly. This teacher knows that sometimes she needs to assign students to groups so that assignments are tailored to student need, but that in other instances, it makes more sense for students to form their own working groups. She sees that some students prefer or benefit from independent work, while others usually fare best with pairs or triads.

In a differentiated classroom, the teacher uses many different group configurations over time, and students experience many different working groups and arrangements. "Fluid" is a good word to describe assignment of students to groups in such a heterogeneous classroom. In the older, "three groups approach" to instruction, student assignment to tasks was more fixed. Flexible grouping will be discussed in greater detail in Chapter 4.

Differentiated instruction is NOT just "tailoring the same suit of clothes."

Many teachers think that they differentiate instruction when they ask some students to answer more complex questions in a discussion or to share advanced information on a topic, grade some students a little harder or easier on an assignment in response to the students' perceived ability and effort, or let students select which questions to answer or skip on a test. Certainly such modifications reflect a teacher's awareness of differences in student profiles and, to that degree, the modifications are movement in the direction of differentiation. While they are not necessarily ineffective or "bad" strategies on the teacher's part, they are a "micro-differentiation" or "tailoring," and are often just not enough.

If the basic assignment itself is far too easy for an advanced learner, having a chance to answer a complex question is not an adequate challenge. If information is essential for a struggling learner, allowing him to skip a test question because he never understood the information is ineffective. If the information in the basic assignment is simply too complex for a learner until she has the chance to assimilate needed background information and skills, being "easier" on her when grading her assignment does not help her in the long run. In sum, trying to stretch a garment that is far too small or attempting to tuck and gather a garment that is far too large is likely to be less effective than getting clothes that are the right fit at a given time.

What Differentiated Instruction Is

Differentiated instruction is PROACTIVE.

In a differentiated classroom, the teacher assumes that different learners have differing needs. Therefore, the teacher proactively plans a variety of ways to "get at" and express learning. He still needs to tailor or fine-tune instruction for individual learners, but because different learning options are available based on his knowledge of varied learner needs, the chances are greater that the learning experiences will provide an appropriate fit for many learners. Effective differentiation will typically be proactively planned by the teacher to be robust enough to address a range of learner needs, in contrast with planning a single approach for everyone and reactively trying to adjust the plans when it becomes apparent that the lesson is not working for some of the learners for whom it was intended.

Differentiated instruction is more QUALITATIVE than quantitative.

Many teachers incorrectly assume that differentiating instruction means giving some students more work to do, and others less. For example, a teacher might assign two book reports to advanced readers and only one to struggling readers. Or a struggling math student might have to do only the computation problems while advanced math students do the word problems as well.

Although such approaches to differentiation may seem to have an adequate rationale, they are typically ineffective. One book report is too much for a struggling learner without additional support in the process of reading as well as interpreting the text. Or a student who could act out the substance of the book effectively might be overwhelmed by writing a three-page report. If writing one book report is "too easy" for the advanced reader, doing "twice as much" of the same thing is not only unlikely to remedy the problem, but it could also seem like punishment. A student who has already demonstrated mastery of one math skill is ready to stop practice related to that skill and begin practice in a subsequent skill. Simply adjusting the *quantity* of an assignment will generally be less effective than adjusting the *nature* of the assignment to match student needs as well.

Differentiated Instruction is ROOTED IN ASSESSMENT.

A teacher who understands the need for teaching and learning to be a good match for students looks for every opportunity to know her students better. She sees conversations with individuals, classroom discussions, student work, observation, and formal assessment as a way to gather just a little more insight about what works for each learner. What she learns becomes a catalyst for crafting instruction in ways that help each student make the most of his potential and talents. Assessment is no longer predominately something that happens at the end of a unit to determine "who got it." Assessment routinely takes place as a unit begins to determine the particular needs of individuals in relation to the unit's goals.

Throughout the unit, in a variety of ways, teachers assess students' developing readiness levels, interests, and modes of learning. Then the teachers design learning experiences based on their best understanding. Culminating products, or other forms of "final" assessment, take many forms, with the goal of finding a way for each student to most successfully share what he or she has learned in the course of the unit.

Differentiated instruction provides MULTIPLE APPROACHES to content, process, and product.

In all classrooms, teachers deal with at least three curricular elements: (1) content—input, what students learn; (2) process—how students go about making sense of ideas and information; and (3) product—output, how students demonstrate what they have learned. These elements are so important in differentiating instruction that they are dealt with in depth in Chapters 8, 9, and 10. By differentiating these three elements, teachers offer different approaches to *what* students learn, *how* they learn it, and how they *demonstrate what they've learned*. What these different approaches have in common, however, is that they are crafted to encourage substantial growth in all students.

Differentiated instruction is STUDENT CENTERED.

Differentiated classrooms operate on the premise that learning experiences are most effective when they are engaging, relevant, and interesting. A corollary to that premise is that all students will not always find the same avenues to learning equally engaging, relevant, and interesting. Further, differentiated instruction acknowledges that later understandings must be built on previous understandings and that not all students possess the same understandings at the outset of a given investigation. Teachers who differentiate instruction in mixed-ability classrooms seek to provide appropriately challenging learning experiences for all their students. These teachers realize that sometimes a task that lacks challenge for some learners is frustratingly complex to others.

In addition, teachers in differentiated classes understand the need to help students take increasing responsibility for their own growth. It's easier sometimes in large classrooms for a teacher to tell students everything rather than guiding them to think on their own, accept significant responsibility for learning, and develop a sense of pride in what they do. In a differentiated classroom, it's necessary for learners to be active in making and evaluating decisions. Teaching students to share responsibility enables a teacher to work with varied groups or individuals for portions of the day. It also prepares students far better for life.

Differentiated instruction is A BLEND of whole-class, group, and individual instruction.

There are times in all classrooms when it is more effective or efficient to share information

or use the same activity with the whole class. Such whole-group instruction establishes common understandings and a sense of community for students by sharing discussion and review. As illustrated in Figure 1.1, the pattern of instruction in a differentiated classroom could be represented by mirror images of a wavy line, with students coming together as a whole group to begin a study, moving out to pursue learning in small groups or individually, coming back together to share and make plans for additional investigation, moving out again for more work, coming together again to share or review, and so on.

Differentiated instruction is "ORGANIC."

In a differentiated classroom, teaching is evolutionary. Students and teachers are learners together. While teachers may know more about the subject matter at hand, they are continuously learning about how their students learn. Ongoing collaboration with students is necessary to refine the learning opportunities so they're effective for each student. Differentiated instruction is dynamic: Teachers monitor the match between learner and learning and make adjustments as warranted. And while teachers are aware that sometimes the learner/learning match is less than ideal, they also understand that they can continually make adjustments. Differentiated instruction often results in more effective matches than does the mode of teaching that insists that one assignment serves all learners well.

Further, a teacher in a differentiated classroom does not classify herself as someone who "already differentiates instruction." Rather, that teacher is fully aware that every hour of teaching, every day in the classroom can reveal one more way to make the classroom a better match for its learners.

Finally, such a teacher does not see differentiation as a strategy or something to do when

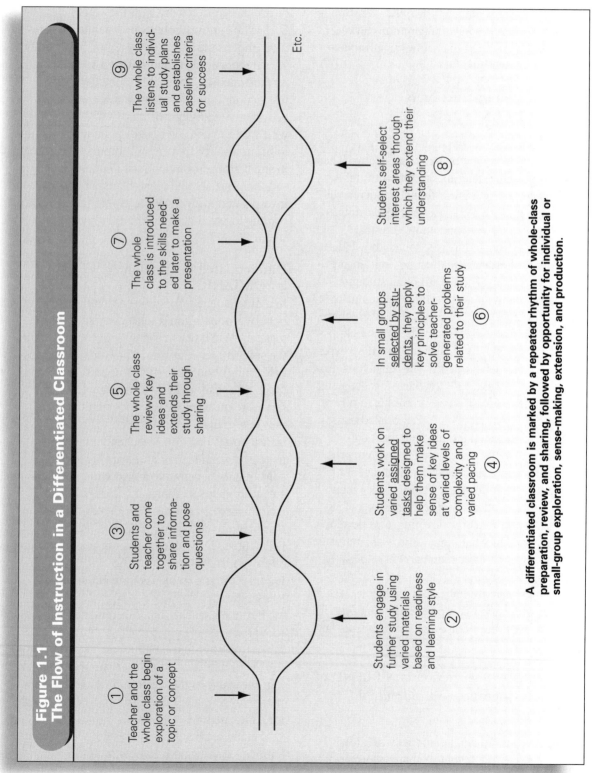

Figure 1.1
The Flow of Instruction in a Differentiated Classroom

① Teacher and the whole class begin exploration of a topic or concept

② Students engage in further study using varied materials based on readiness and learning style

③ Students and teacher come together to share information and pose questions

④ Students work on varied assigned tasks designed to help them make sense of key ideas at varied levels of complexity and varied pacing

⑤ The whole class reviews key ideas and extends their study through sharing

⑥ In small groups selected by students, they apply key principles to solve teacher-generated problems related to their study

⑦ The whole class is introduced to the skills needed later to make a presentation

⑧ Students self-select interest areas through which they extend their understanding

⑨ The whole class listens to individual study plans and establishes baseline criteria for success

Etc.

A differentiated classroom is marked by a repeated rhythm of whole-class preparation, review, and sharing, followed by opportunity for individual or small-group exploration, sense-making, extension, and production.

there's extra time. Rather, it is a way of life in the classroom. She does not seek or follow a recipe for differentiation, but rather combines what she can learn about differentiation from a range of sources to her own professional instincts and knowledge base to do whatever it takes to reach out to each learner.

A New Image to Keep in Mind

As you continue reading about how to differentiate instruction in mixed-ability classrooms, keep this new image in mind:

In a differentiated classroom, the teacher proactively plans and carries out varied approaches to content, process, and product in anticipation of and response to student differences in readiness, interest, and learning needs.

❦ ❦ ❦

The practical strategies in this book should crystallize this new image for you as you work at differentiating instruction in your classroom.

THE Rationale FOR Differentiated Instruction IN Mixed-Ability Classrooms

Some educators say a "good" education is one that ensures that all students learn certain core information and master certain basic competencies according to a prescribed route and time line. Others define a "good" education as one that helps students maximize their capacity as learners. Because the latter definition encourages continual lifting of ceilings and testing of personal limits, it would seem to make the best sense for all learners.

How People Best Learn: The Engine That Drives Effective Differentiation

We actually know a great deal about how people learn. For example, we know that each learner must make meaning of what teachers seek to teach. We know that the meaning-making process is influenced by the student's prior understandings, interests, beliefs, how the student learns best, and the student's attitudes about self and school (National Research Council, 1990).

We also know that learning takes place most effectively in classrooms where knowledge is clearly and powerfully organized, students are highly active in the learning process, assessments are rich and varied, and students feel a sense of safety and connection (National Research Council, 1990; Wiggins & McTighe, 1998).

We know that learning happens best when a learning experience pushes the learner a bit beyond his or her independence level. When a student continues to work on understandings and skills already mastered, little if any new learning takes place. On the other hand, if tasks are far ahead of a student's current point of mastery, frustration results and learning does not (Howard, 1994; Vygotsky, 1962).

In addition, we know that motivation to learn increases when we feel a kinship with, interest in, or passion for what we are attempting to learn (Piaget, 1978). Further, we go about learning in a wide variety of ways, influenced by how our individual brains are wired, our culture, and our gender (Delpit, 1995; Gardner, 1983; Heath, 1983; Sternberg, 1985; Sullivan, 1993).

In the end, we can draw at least three powerful conclusions about teaching and learning. First, while the image of a "standard issue" student is comfortable, it denies most of what we know about the wide variance that inevitably exists within any group of learners. Second, there is no substitute for high-quality curriculum and instruction in classrooms. Third, even in the presence of high-quality curriculum and instruction, we will fall woefully short of the goal of helping each learner build a good life through the power of education unless we build bridges between the learner and learning.

These three conclusions are the engine that drives effective differentiation. They, along with our best knowledge of what makes learning happen, are nonnegotiables in a classroom where a teacher sets out to make each learner a captive of the mystery and power of knowing about the world in which those learners will live out their lives.

Mixed-ability classrooms that are ambiguous about learning goals, that evoke little passion, that cast the teacher as the centerpiece of learning, and that lack responsiveness to student variance show little understanding of these various learning realities. They lack the foundation of all powerful learning, top quality curriculum and instruction—as well as a key refinement of superior curriculum and instruction, differentiated or responsive instruction. In regard to the first-named deficit, these classrooms operate as though clarity of understanding can be achieved through ambiguity and that fires of inquiry will be ignited in the absence of a flame. In regard to the latter deficit, they imply that all students

need to learn the same things in the same way over the same time span.

Ensuring rock solid clarity about where we want students to end up as a result of a sequence of learning is fundamental to educational success. Remembering that we cannot reach the mind we do not engage ought to be a daily compass for educational planning. Offering multiple and varied avenues to learning is a hallmark of the kind of professional quality that denotes expertise. Our students—each of them—is a message that we can never stop attending to the craftsmanship and artistry of teaching.

The focus of this book is on the refinement of high-quality, alluring instruction that we call "differentiation." This book, however, calls for clarity and quality in what we differentiate. It is an exercise in futility to try to meet the needs of learners by low quality, incoherent approaches to differentiation. They provide learners with several varieties of gruel. They will fall short for virtually all students.

Looking at a Classroom Through Many Eyes

Their teacher cares about her work. She likes kids and she likes teaching. She works hard and is proud of her profession. The kids know that, and they like her for all those things. But the day seems long too often for many of the students. Sometimes their teacher knows it. Often she does not.

Lin does not understand English. No one understands her language either as far as she can tell. The teacher smiles at her and assigned a classmate to help her. That classmate does not speak her language. The classmate smiles too. Sometimes smiles help. Sometimes they seem like music without sound. In math, Lin understands more. Numbers carry fewer hidden meanings than words. No one expects her to understand, however, and so no one asks her to go to the board and work problems. That's okay, because if she went, she wouldn't have words to tell about her numbers.

Rafael wants to read aloud, wants to ask for more books about the people in history, wants to add his questions to the ones the other kids ask in discussions. He doesn't. His friends are down on school. They say it's not for them—not for kids like him. Learning belongs to another kind of person, they say. Where would grades get him? they ask. Maybe they're right. He knows he won't go to college or get a big deal job—but he secretly thinks about it. And he wants to know things. But it's hard to ask.

Serena reads her mom's books at home. She reads the magazine that comes with the Sunday *Times*. She and her friends write and produce a neighborhood play every summer. Lots of people come. In school, she's learning 4th grade spelling words. She gets *A*'s on the tests. She gets *A*'s on everything. She doesn't work hard like when she's getting the plays ready. In school, she feels dishonest. She makes up stories in her head while she waits for other students to learn. They try hard and don't get *A*'s. That makes her feel dishonest too.

Trevor hates reading. He misbehaves sometimes, but it's not that he wants to. He's just tired of seeming stupid in front of everyone. He thinks he sounds worst in the class when he reads aloud. The odd thing is that he understands what the pages are about when somebody else reads them. How can you understand what you can't read? And how can you be a normal 4th grader and not be able to read?

Lesley knows she doesn't learn like the other kids do. She knows people think she's "slow." She has a special teacher who comes to class to help her, or takes her to a special room to learn things. She likes that teacher. She likes her main teacher too. She doesn't like the fact that having two teachers makes her feel different. She doesn't like the fact that what she studies seems so unlike what everyone else studies. She doesn't like feeling like she's on the edge of the action all the time.

Danny likes coming to school because people don't yell there all the time. Nobody hits at school—or if they do, they get in trouble. There are things to play with at school. His teacher smiles. She says she's glad he's there. He's not sure why. He doesn't do well. He wants to, but it's hard to concentrate. He worries about his mom. He worries about his sister. He forgets to listen. At home, it's hard to do homework. He gets behind.

Theo keeps listening for questions that sound like something a person in his house would ask. He keeps listening for language that sounds like his. He keeps waiting for a signal that the people he studies in school have some connection with him. He keeps waiting to see how the knowledge fits in with his neighborhood. He doesn't mind learning. He just wants to know why. He's restless.

Their teacher works hard on preparing their lessons. They know that. Sometimes—many times—it seems like she's teaching lessons, not kids. Sometimes it seems like she thinks they are all one person. Sometimes it's like they are synonyms for test scores. Sometimes school is like a shoe that's shaped for somebody else's foot.

Perhaps a good way to begin an exploration of differentiated teaching is to look at the classroom through the eyes of two broad categories of students—those who are advanced and those who struggle. Those two categories, of course, encompass many different sorts of students, but they do at least provide a place to begin thinking about the readiness of academically diverse learners and the range of needs they bring to school. In later chapters we'll look at needs related to student interest and learning profile.

Understanding the Needs of Advanced Learners

Whatever label we use—"gifted learners," "high-end learners," "academically talented learners," or "advanced learners"—it seems to bother many people. In this book, "advanced learners" is used for two reasons. First, this label doesn't seem to carry some of the more controversial overtones of some other descriptors. Second, it says to the teacher in a mixed-ability classroom, "Don't worry so much about identification processes and formal labeling. Take a look at who is ahead of where you and the curriculum guide expect your students to be. Then you have a place to start."

Some students may be advanced in September and not in May—or in May, but not in September. Some may be advanced in math, but not in reading; or in lab work, but not in memorization of related scientific formulas. Some may be advanced for a short time, others throughout their lives but only in certain endeavors. Some learners are consistently advanced in many areas.

Because the primary intent of differentiated instruction is to maximize student capacity, when you can see (or you have a hunch) that a student can learn more deeply, move at a brisker pace, or make more connections than instructional blueprints might suggest, that's a good time to offer advanced learning opportunities.

But advanced learners, like other learners, need help in developing their abilities. Without teachers that coach for growth and curriculums that are appropriately challenging, these learners may fail to achieve their potential. For example, when a recent study compared Advanced Placement Exam results of the top 1 percent of U.S. students with top students in 13 other countries, U.S. students scored last in biology, 11th in chemistry, and 9th in physics

(Ross, 1993). There are many reasons why advanced learners don't achieve their full potential.

• **Advanced learners can become mentally lazy, even though they do well in school.** We have evidence (Clark, 1992; Ornstein & Thompson, 1984; Wittrock, 1977) that a brain loses capacity and "tone" without vigorous use, in much the same way that a little-used muscle does. If a student produces "success" without effort, potential brainpower can be lost.

• **Advanced learners may become "hooked" on the trappings of success.** They may think grades are more important than ideas, being praised is more important than taking intellectual risks, and being right is more valuable than making new discoveries. Unfortunately, many advanced learners quickly learn to do what is "safe" or what "pays," rather than what could result in greater long-term learning.

• **Advanced learners may become perfectionists.** We praise them for being the best readers, assign them to help others who can't get the math, and compliment them when they score highest on tests. When people get excited about their performance, these students often assume it's possible to keep being the best. Because they attach so much of their self-worth to the rewards of schooling and because those rewards are accessible for years at a time, advanced learners often don't learn to struggle or fail. Failure then becomes something to avoid at all costs. Some advanced learners develop compulsive behaviors, from excessive worry to procrastination to eating disorders, and occasionally even suicide. Many advanced learners simply become less productive and less satisfied. Creative production typically has a high failure-to-success ratio. Students who have the capacity to be producers of new knowledge but who are afraid of failure are unlikely to see their productive capacity realized.

• **Advanced learners may fail to develop a sense of self-efficacy.** Self-esteem is fostered by being told you are important, valued, or successful. Self-efficacy, by contrast, comes from stretching yourself to achieve a goal that you first believed was beyond your reach. Although many advanced learners easily achieve a sort of hollow self-esteem, they never develop a sense of self-efficacy. These students often go through life feeling like impostors, fearfully awaiting the inevitable day the world will discover they aren't so capable after all.

• **Advanced learners may fail to develop study and coping skills.** When students coast through school with only modest effort, they may look successful. In fact, however, success in life typically follows persistence, hard work, and risk. In many cases, advanced learners make good grades without learning to work hard. Then when hard work is required, they become frightened, resentful, or frustrated. In addition, they "succeed" without having to learn to study or grapple with ideas or persist in the face of uncertainty. We graduate many highly able students with "evidence" that success requires minimal effort, and without the skills necessary to achieve when they discover that evidence is invalid.

Advanced learners, like all learners, need learning experiences designed to fit them. When teachers are not sensitive to that need, they may set learning goals for advanced students that are too low or that develop new skills too infrequently. Then, if students are successful anyhow, they often fail to develop the desirable balance between running into walls and scaling them. Advanced learners share other learners' need for teachers who can help them set high goals, devise plans for reaching those goals, tolerate frustrations and share joys along the way, and sight new horizons after each accomplishment.

Several key principles are useful when coaching advanced learners for growth.

• Continually raise the ceilings of expectations so that advanced learners are competing with their own possibilities rather than with a norm.

• Make clear what would constitute excellence for the advanced learner so she knows, at least in large measure, what to aim for in her work.

• As you raise ceilings of expectation, raise the support system available to the student to reach his goals. When tasks are appropriately challenging, you'll find high-end learners need your support and scaffolding to achieve genuine success, just as other learners do.

• Be sure to balance rigor and joy in learning. It's difficult to imagine a talented learner persisting when there is little pleasure in what the learner once thought was fascinating. It's also difficult to imagine growth toward expertise when there is all joy and no rigor.

Understanding the Needs of Struggling Learners

Labels are tricky with struggling learners, too. The term "slow learners" often carries with it a negative connotation of being shiftless or lazy, yet many struggling learners work hard and conscientiously—especially when tasks are neither boring (such as a steady diet of drill and skill) nor anxiety-producing (such as tasks that require more than they can deliver even when they work hard). The term "at-risk" overlooks the portion of the learner that may well be "at-promise." One child's struggle stems from a learning disability, another's home life takes all her energy, and another just finds a subject his nemesis.

Further, just like with an advanced learner, the learning profile of a struggling learner may shift over time; for example, suddenly a student becomes an eager reader after trailing the class in decoding and comprehension for some time. Many students whom we perceive to be "slow," "at-risk," or "struggling," may actually be quite proficient in talents that schools often treat as secondary, such as leadership among neighborhood peers, story telling, or building contraptions out of discarded materials.

Nonetheless, many students do struggle with school tasks. They are a diverse group who can challenge the artistry of the most expert teacher in listening deeply, believing unconditionally, and moving beyond a recipe or blueprint approach to teaching to shape classrooms that offer many avenues and timetables to understanding.

Here are some principles that can be helpful in ensuring that struggling learners maximize their capacity in school.

• **Look for the struggling learner's positives.** Every student does some things relatively well. It's important to find those things, to affirm them in private conversations and before peers, to design tasks that draw on those strengths, and to ensure that the student can use strengths as a means of tackling areas of difficulty. A student with kinesthetic ability and a weakness in reading, for example, may find it easier to comprehend a story by pantomiming the events in it as someone else reads aloud, and *then* reading the story to herself.

• **Don't let what's broken extinguish what works.** Few adults elect to spend the majority of their days practicing what they *can't* do. The difference between us and students is that we have a choice. Struggling learners are more likely to retain motivation to learn when their days allow them to concentrate on tasks that are relevant and make them feel powerful. Many

learning-disabled gifted learners, for example, find school intolerable because educators spend so much time "remediating" their flaws that there's no space for enhancing their strengths. It's important to avoid this temptation with struggling learners in general.

• **Pay attention to relevance.** It's easy to understand why many struggling learners believe school is not "their place." They don't "do school" well today, and we keep insisting that persistence will pay off "someday"—often in another grade or level of school in which the child believes he has little prospect for success. Dewey (1938) reminds us that if school isn't for today, it will often turn out to be for nothing. He believed this to be true for all learners. Certainly it is so for many struggling learners. A skilled teacher conscientiously works to make each day's explorations compelling for that day.

• **Go for powerful learning.** If struggling learners can't learn everything, make sure they learn the big ideas, key concepts, and governing principles of the subject at hand. Not only does this approach help struggling learners see the big picture of the topic and subject, but it also helps build a scaffolding of meaning, a requisite framework for future success.

• **Teach up.** Know your struggling students' learning profiles. Create tasks for struggling learners (individuals or groups with similar profiles) that are a chunk more difficult than you believe they can accomplish. Then teach for success (by encouraging, providing support, guiding planning, delineating criteria, and so on.) so that the seemingly unattainable moves within the learners' reach. A strong sense of self-efficacy comes not from being told we're terrific, but rather from our own recognition that we've accomplished something we believed was beyond us.

• **Use many avenues to learning.** Some students learn best with their ears, some with their eyes, some with touch or movement. Some are solitary learners, some must interact with friends in order to learn. Some students work well by gathering details and constructing a bird's-eye view of what is being studied. Others will not learn unless the bird's-eye view is clear to them before they encounter the details. Struggling learners sometimes become more successful learners just because their way of learning is readily accessible through both teacher design and student choice.

• **See with the eyes of love.** Some kids come at the world with their dukes up. Life is a fight for them in part because the belligerence that surrounds them spawns belligerence in them. These kids are no less difficult for a teacher to embrace than for the rest of the world. But behind the tension and combativeness abundant in the world of the angry child, what's lacking is the acceptance and affection he disinvites. Perhaps a good definition of a friend is someone who loves us as we are, and envisions us as we might be. If so, these students need a teacher who is a friend. The eyes of love reflect both unconditional acceptance and unwavering vision of total potential. It's not easy, but it is critical.

Here are a few important principles to recall as you plan for success for students who struggle with school.

• Be clear on what students must know, understand, and be able to do in order to grow in their grasp of a subject. Teacher fog will only obscure an already difficult view for struggling students.

• Set important goals of understanding and use of ideas for struggling students, then figure out how to build scaffolding leading to student success in those goals. Don't dilute the goals.

• Work for learning-in-context. In other words, help the student see how ideas and skills are part of their own families and neighborhoods and futures. Helping students connect their lives with ideas and skills presupposes that, as teachers, we understand the students' neighborhoods, cultures, and families and what connections are possible.

• Plan teaching and learning through many modalities. If a student has heard about an idea, sung about it, built a representation of it, and read about it, success is far more likely than if one avenue to learning predominates.

• Continually find ways to let the student know that you believe in him or her—and reinforce legitimate success whenever it happens. If I believe in you, I'll find a way to ensure that you succeed, and will be sure to point out that success to you whenever it is genuine and earned.

Differentiating Learning Experiences to Address Academic Diversity

Differentiated instruction is not simply giving a "normal" assignment to most students and "different" assignments to students who are struggling or advanced. That approach usually creates a "pecking order" among students, which then tends to cause other troubles. Students assigned a remedial assignment, which looks simple to others, can take it as a message that they are inferior. Advanced assignments tend to look more interesting to nearly everyone except the advanced learner, who may perceive it as more work. These strategies can backfire, causing both advanced and struggling students to feel different from those who do the "real" assignment.

In a differentiated classroom, a number of things are going on in any given class period. Over time, all students complete assignments individually and in small groups, and whole-group instruction occurs as well. Sometimes students select their group size and tasks, sometimes they are assigned. Sometimes the teacher establishes criteria for success, sometimes students do. And setting standards for success is often a collaborative process. Because there are many different things happening, no one assignment defines "normal," and no one "sticks out." The teacher thinks and plans in terms of "multiple avenues to learning" for varied needs, rather than in terms of "normal" and "different." The goal for each student is maximum growth from his current "learning position." The goal of the teacher is coming to understand more and more about that learning position so that learning matches learner need.

A Final Thought

In the end, all learners need your energy, your heart, and your mind. They have that in common because they are young humans. *How* they need you, however, differs. Unless we understand and respond to those differences, we fail many learners.

Some of us are drawn to teach struggling learners, some are natural champions of advanced learners, and some have an affinity for the sort of "standard" student who matches our image of the 4th or 8th or 11th grader we thought we'd be teaching. That we have preferences is, again, human. The most effective teachers spend a career meticulously cultivating their appreciation for children not so easy for them to automatically embrace, while continuing to draw energy from those students whom they more automatically find delightful.

THE Role OF THE Teacher IN A Differentiated Classroom

Mixed-ability class-rooms that offer differentiated instruction make good sense for teachers, as well as students. For many teachers, though, offering differentiated instruction first requires a paradigm shift.

The Teacher's Role in a Differentiated Classroom

Teachers who become comfortable with differentiated classrooms would probably say their role differs in some significant ways from that of a more traditional teacher. When teachers differentiate instruction, they move away from seeing themselves as keepers and dispensers of knowledge and move toward seeing themselves as *organizers of learning opportunities*. While content knowledge remains important, these teachers focus less on knowing all the answers, and focus more on "reading their students." They

then create ways to learn that both capture students' attention and lead to understanding. Organizing a class for effective activity and exploration becomes the highest priority.

Teachers who differentiate instruction focus on their role as *coach* or *mentor*, give students as much responsibility for learning as they can handle, and teach them to handle a little more. These teachers grow in their ability to (1) assess student readiness through a variety of means, (2) "read" and interpret student clues about interests and learning preferences, (3) create a variety of ways students can gather information and ideas, (4) develop varied ways students can explore and "own" ideas, and (5) present varied channels through which students can express and expand understandings. "Covering information" takes a back seat to making meaning out of important ideas. Most of us have not been trained to look at teaching in this light, but we are learners, too. We may not be able to transform our image of ourselves in a flash, but we can change over the course of a career.

Best Practice Accounts for Varied Learners

Differentiation calls on a teacher to realize that classrooms must be places where teachers pursue our best understandings of teaching and learning every day, and also to recall daily that no practice is truly best practice unless it works for the individual learner.

For instance, most of us who teach know that a lesson that "hooks" students has many merits. Differentiation affirms that principle, but reminds us that what may "hook" one student might well puzzle, bore, or irritate others. Differentiation doesn't suggest that a teacher can be all things to all individuals all the time. It does, however, mandate that a teacher create a reasonable range of approaches to learning much of the time, so that most students find learning a fit much of the time.

Ron Brandt (1998) offers a number of characteristics for what he calls powerful learning. Figure 3.1 offers a few of these "best-practice" principles, as well as corollaries that remind us that truly expert teaching is inevitably differentiated. Making the link between best practice teaching and differentiation helps set the stage for understanding the role of the teacher in a differentiated classroom.

Learning to Lead a Differentiated Classroom

Few of us as teachers automatically know how to lead a classroom that responds to the daunting reality of learner variance. It is a learned skill, in the same sense of any other art or craft. Perhaps a good place to begin is by listing some key skills that a teacher will develop over time as she consciously and reflectively works on differentiating instruction. Teachers who become comfortable and competent with differentiation almost inevitably develop skills of:

- organizing and focusing curriculum on essential information, understandings, and skills,
- seeing and reflecting on individuals as well as the group,
- hunting for insights about individuals,
- peeling back first impressions, looking beyond actions, erasing stereotypes,
- giving students a voice,
- thinking of and using time flexibly,
- scrounging for a wide range of materials,
- thinking of many ways to accomplish a common goal,
- diagnosing student need and crafting learning experiences in response to diagnoses,
- thinking of what could go wrong in an activity or task and structuring student work to avoid potential problems,
- sharing responsibility for teaching and learning with students, ensuring that students are prepared for the shared roles,
- moving students among varied work arrangements as a way to see students in new ways and to help them see themselves in new ways,
- keeping track of student proximity to and growth toward personal and group benchmarks,
- organizing materials and space,
- giving directions,
- teaching for success, and
- building a sense of community in the classroom.

Three metaphors for the role of the teacher in a differentiated classroom are helpful. (Feel free to create your own metaphor as well.)

The Teacher as Director of the Orchestra. This metaphor generates the image of a leader who knows the music intimately, can interpret it elegantly, can pull together a group of people who may not know each other well to achieve a common end, even though they all play differ-

FIGURE 3.1
Best-Practice Teaching Linked with Differentiation

Best Practice (Brandt, 1998): People learn best under these conditions:	Differentiation: We need to attend to student differences because...
1. What they learn is personally meaningful.	Because students have different backgrounds and interest, there's no guarantee that they'll all find the same things personally meaningful.
2. What they learn is challenging, and they accept the challenge.	Because students learn at different rates, a pace, text, or task that challenges some students will frustrate or bore others.
3. What they learn is appropriate to their developmental level.	At any time some students will think more concretely and some more abstractly, some more dependently and others more independently.
4. They can learn in their own way, have choices, and feel in control.	It's a sure bet students won't all opt to learn in the same way, make the same choices, or feel in control with the same parameters.
5. They use what they know to construct new knowledge.	Because they don't all know the same things at the same degree of competency, students will construct knowledge differently.
6. They have opportunities for social interaction.	Students will vary in the amount of collaboration they need and the sorts of peers with whom they work best.
7. They get helpful feedback.	What is helpful feedback for one student may not be for another.
8. They acquire and use strategies.	Each student needs to acquire strategies new to that student and use them in ways that are personally helpful.
9. They experience a positive emotional climate.	Classrooms that are quite positive for some students are distinctly not so for others.
10. The environment supports the intended learning.	Students will need varied scaffolding to achieve both common and personal goals.

Note: "Best Practice" column adapted from: Brandt, R. (1998). *Powerful learning.* Alexandria, VA: Association for Supervision and Curriculum Development.

ent instruments. There's a time in rehearsals for individual practice, a time for sectional practice, and a time for the whole group to work together. There's a need to polish the performance of each individual musician so that the work of the whole is of quality. In the end, each musician contributes to a meaningful performance and earns the applause (or scorn) of the audience. The director of the orchestra helps musicians make music, but does not make the music himself.

The Teacher as Coach. A good coach has clear goals for the team, but also for every individual on the team. Practices will likely involve some common activities, but will also likely call on each player to improve areas of weakness and polish areas of strength. The coach is generally part psychologist, having to understand what motivates each player and use that understanding to get the player to sweat and even risk pain in order to develop his skill. Also, however, the coach must build a team spirit that transcends individual concerns. The coach is incredibly active during both practices and games—running the sidelines, motivating, giving directions, calling small groups aside at key times for strategy adjustments. The coach, however, does not play the game.

The Teacher as Jazz Musician. Improvisation combines with a high level of musical competence to enable the jazz musician to think both inside and outside the box. The jazz musician has the big picture, but can add new notes, change tempo, step back for a soloist to assume the spotlight, or become the soloist in the spotlight. A piece becomes longer or shorter, more plaintive, or more playful as the mood of the group dictates. It is the artistry and confidence of the jazz musician with the music, instrument, and group that allow her to abandon the score for the sake of the music, the group, and the audience. A good differentiated classroom is jazz!

Differentiating Instruction: Rules of Thumb

Before looking at specific ways to modify content, process, and product for students in your mixed-ability classroom, it helps to understand several general guidelines that make differentiation possible.

• **Be clear on the key concepts and generalizations or principles that give meaning and structure to the topic, chapter, unit, or lesson you are planning.** Few learners can amass and recall scores of bits of data on multiple topics, let alone organize and use all that data. All learners would probably fare better if lessons focused on key ideas and meanings. When the curriculum "covers" 500 pages, it is difficult to do much more than drag everyone through those pages in the time available. On the other hand, focusing on key concepts and generalizations can ensure that all learners gain powerful understandings that serve as building blocks for meaning and access to other knowledge. Key concepts act as springboards to help all learners make connections between the topic under consideration and expanded studies. And these learners are more likely to find their school experiences more memorable, useful, and engaging. It's often useful to begin planning with knowledge, understandings, and skills you want individuals and the group to have mastered when a unit concludes, then take a step by step journey "backwards" to figure out the best progression you and the students can take in order to reach the destination.

• **Think of assessment as a road map for your thinking and planning.** School often casts assessment as a test. In fact, everything a student does, from an oral contribution in a discussion to a homework assignment to completion of an interest checklist, is a form of assessment. When you begin to see the wide array of assessment sources in the classroom, you begin to see how many ways there are to learn about learners. School often casts assessment as something that happens at the end of a unit to see who "got it" and who didn't. In fact, assessment is most useful when it comes at the outset of a unit or along the way in the unit. At those points, assessment invites us to adjust our teaching based on current information. School often casts assessment as dependent on reading and writing. While those are essential skills for most roles in life, they are not always the best way to find out what all learners have come to understand and be able to do as the result of a learning sequence. Fruitful assessment often poses the question, "What is an array of ways I can offer students to demonstrate their understanding and skills?" In that way, assessment becomes a part of teaching for success and a way to extend rather than merely measure learning.

• **Lessons for all students should emphasize critical and creative thinking.** In the imperfect world of teaching, you may not always accomplish this, but it should be your clear goal. In other words, it is not acceptable for remedial students to do "low-level" tasks that require only memorization of information and minimal comprehension. All tasks should require that students, at the very least, understand and be able to apply the meaning of the ideas at hand. Much of the time, all students should be called on to use information, understandings, and skills to solve knotty problems that defy a recipe-like answer. Some students may need more support than others to make and back an argument, for example. Some may benefit from using more advanced research materials as they construct their argument. Some may profit from a minilesson that recaps how to make and support a solid argument. Some may need to develop their arguments orally and have

their work written by a peer or adult. Some may need to use materials in a language other than English, or write initially in a first language and then translate into English. But if argumentation is a valuable skill, all students should engage in it with appropriate scaffolding.

• **Lessons for all students should be engaging.** Again, you may not always achieve that goal, but it should still be something to strive for as a measure of growth as an educator. Although all students will sometimes have to do drill and practice to accumulate needed data, it is not acceptable for struggling learners to spend most of their time trying to master basic information while other students get to use it. In fact, we now know (Means, Chelemer, & Knapp, 1991) that many learners who struggle would find learning more natural and sensible if they were consistently presented with problems, issues, dilemmas, and unknowns that required them to use more of what they have learned.

• **In a differentiated classroom, there should be a balance between student-selected and teacher-assigned tasks and working arrangements.** This balance will vary somewhat for each student, based on the student's maturity, the nature of the task, classroom conditions, and so on. But all students should regularly have choices to make, and all students should regularly be matched with tasks compatible with their individual learner profile. Again, struggling students should not typically work alone on a teacher-assigned task while other students typically work together on tasks of their own choice.

❦ ❦ ❦

The next chapter provides an overview of learning environments most likely to be hospitable to a philosophy of differentiation.

THE Learning Environment
IN A Differentiated Classroom

The tone of any classroom greatly affects those who inhabit it and the learning that takes place there. Classroom environment in a setting that strives for differentiation is, if anything, even more of a factor in shaping success. A differentiated classroom should support, and is supported by, an evolving community of learners. What that means is that the teacher leads his students in developing the sorts of attitudes, beliefs, and practices that would characterize a really good neighborhood.

Characteristics of an Effective Learning Community

An effective community of learners is characterized by traits such as the following.

•**Everyone feels welcomed and contributes to everyone else feeling welcomed.** Many things make students feel welcomed. Certainly the direct and positive attention of the teacher is welcoming. Peers who acknowledge the presence of all of their classmates in positive ways should be an expectation. A room that contains student work and other artifacts that are student designed and interesting to look at and think about are inviting. Flexible and comfortable seating options provide a kind of welcome as well. A time in the day when students and teacher can talk about the day, or life in general, builds bridges between learning and the world of the learner. Think about the things that make you feel welcomed—or have the opposite effect—at a neighbor's house, in a store, when you enter the place you work, and so on. It makes a difference to know that the classroom is a place where you feel you belong, because everyone else feels that too. Remember, too, that a part of feeling genuinely welcomed in a place is that key people make an enduring and sustained effort to get to know and understand you.

•**Mutual respect is a nonnegotiable.** It will never be the case that we like or understand everyone with whom we spend time. On the other hand, the classroom is a better place if we learn that everyone shares a need for some common feelings such as acceptance, respect, security, success, and so on. It is a powerful life lesson that regardless of our gender, culture, speed of learning, language, dress, and personality we all feel pain, joy, doubt, triumph—the human emotions. Our lives are made better when they are treated as valuable and worthy of respect. In a differentiated classroom, the teacher helps students distinguish between feelings about something someone did and the value of that person. Further, the teacher helps students learn to solve problems in constructive ways that attend to the issue at hand without making a person or group feel smaller. Respect seldom happens without the cultivation of effort. The teacher is inevitably the catalyst for that effort. It's important to remember that humor plays a central role in a welcoming and respectful classroom. Sarcasm and sharp words do not.

•**Students feel safe in the classroom.** Not only does safety presuppose the absence of physical danger, it requires the absence of emotional danger as well. Students in a differentiated classroom should know it's a good thing to ask for help when it's needed, that it's fine to say you don't know, that an earnest question will get an earnest response, that eyes will not roll when someone expresses something that seems unusual or evident, that fledgling ideas will be given a chance to develop, and so on. Safety means that when I try a new skill, expend

effort, or take a risk with a creative idea, I won't be thought of as foolish or stupid. Safety happens when you feel accepted as you are, and valued enough so that people want to help you become even better.

•**There is a pervasive expectation of growth.** The goal in a differentiated classroom is to help every learner grow as much as he or she can in both general ability and specific talents. The teacher gets excited about the growth of each individual learner, and of the class as a whole. Students learn to chart their own growth and to talk about both their learning goals and ways of achieving them. All growth is worthy of note. One student's growth may mean that the concept of fractions is finally beginning to make sense, while another's growth may reflect an insight about connections between fractions, decimals, and subtraction. In a differentiated classroom, the growth of each of the students is a matter of celebration, and one person's growth is not more or less valuable than another's.

•**The teacher teaches for success.** Sometimes school is characterized by a sort of "gotcha" teaching, in which the game seems to be seeing if the teacher can ask a question or design a test item that will trip up students. In a differentiated classroom, it's the teacher's goal to figure out where a student is in relation to key learning goals and then provide learning experiences that will push the learner a little further and faster than is comfortable. When the learner gives the work a really good effort, the teacher will ensure that there is support necessary to assist the student in reaching the goal that seemed a bit out of reach. That kind of assistance is often called "scaffolding." Figure 4.1 lists some common kinds of scaffolding in classrooms. Scaffolding is whatever kind of assistance is needed for any student to move from prior knowledge and skill to the next level of knowledge and skill. In a good differentiated

FIGURE 4.1
Scaffolding: Providing Support Needed for a Student to Succeed in Challenging Work

- Directions that give more structure—or less
- Tape recorders to help with reading or writing beyond the student's grasp
- Icons to help interpret print
- Reteaching/Extended teaching
- Modeling
- Clear criteria for success
- Reading buddies (with appropriate directions)
- Double-entry journals (at appropriate challenge level)
- Text-survey type strategies
- Teaching through multiple modes
- Use of manipulatives (when needed)
- Gearing reading materials to student reading level
- Use of study guides
- Use of organizers
- New American Lecture

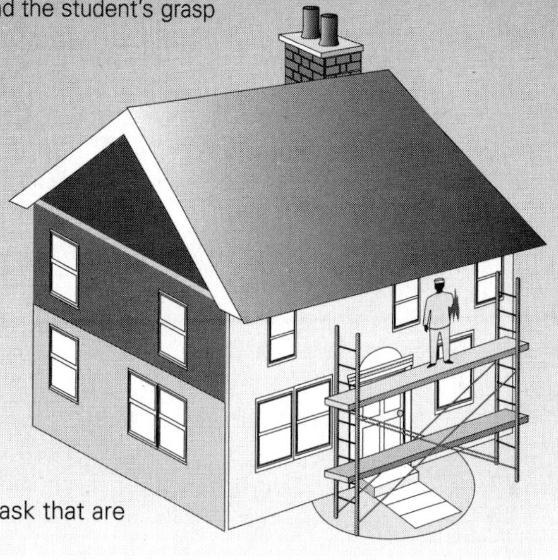

Note: "Challenging work" means assignments or task that are slightly beyond the student's comfort zone.

classroom, the teacher is constantly raising the stakes for success for any individual, then doing whatever is necessary to help the student succeed in taking the next step. Remember that everyone's next step will not be identical, and that every student needs scaffolding in order to stretch.

•**A new sort of fairness is evident.** We often define fair in a classroom as treating everyone alike. In a differentiated classroom, fairness is redefined. In this sort of environment, fair means trying to make sure each student gets what she needs in order to grow and succeed. Students and teacher alike are part of the team trying to ensure that the classroom works well for everyone in the class.

•**Teacher and students collaborate for mutual growth and success.** In a differentiated classroom, just as in a large family, everyone has to take extra responsibility both for their own well-being and for the well-being of others. In this sort of setting, while the teacher is clearly the leader of the group, students can help develop routines for the classroom, make major contributions toward solving problems and refining routines, help one another, keep track of their work, and so on. Different students will be ready for differing amounts of responsibility at any given time, but all students need to be guided in assuming a growing degree of responsibility and independence as a learner and member of a community of learners. Not only is that essential in a differentiated classroom, but it's a huge part of success in life as well.

The teacher sets the tone for the classroom environment. It is a heavy responsibility and a wonderful opportunity to help students shape

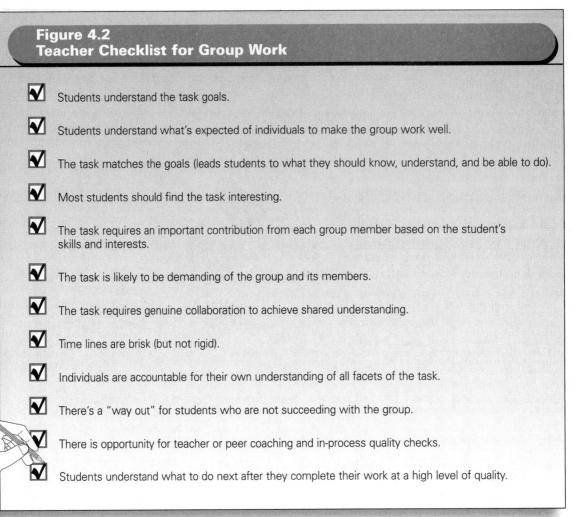

Figure 4.2
Teacher Checklist for Group Work

☑ Students understand the task goals.

☑ Students understand what's expected of individuals to make the group work well.

☑ The task matches the goals (leads students to what they should know, understand, and be able to do).

☑ Most students should find the task interesting.

☑ The task requires an important contribution from each group member based on the student's skills and interests.

☑ The task is likely to be demanding of the group and its members.

☑ The task requires genuine collaboration to achieve shared understanding.

☑ Time lines are brisk (but not rigid).

☑ Individuals are accountable for their own understanding of all facets of the task.

☑ There's a "way out" for students who are not succeeding with the group.

☑ There is opportunity for teacher or peer coaching and in-process quality checks.

☑ Students understand what to do next after they complete their work at a high level of quality.

positive lives. Teachers, as all people, have good days and ones they'd rather not duplicate. While none of us will ever do everything in the way of building a positive classroom environment exactly like we'd have chosen to do it if we could have scripted events, we can get better and better at modeling what we want students to learn—joy in work, pleasure in one another, patience, kindness, and a big heart. Those things help students construct sturdier and more rewarding lives. Working toward them helps the teacher become a wiser person and better professional as well.

Paving the Way for Respect and Success

There are two concrete pieces of guidance that contribute to a positive learning environment in a differentiated classroom that round out the more philosophical guidance offered above. Both suggest students in a differentiated classroom need to collaborate successfully.

•**Continually coach students to be contributing members of a group.** As teachers, we often work in isolation. When that is the case,

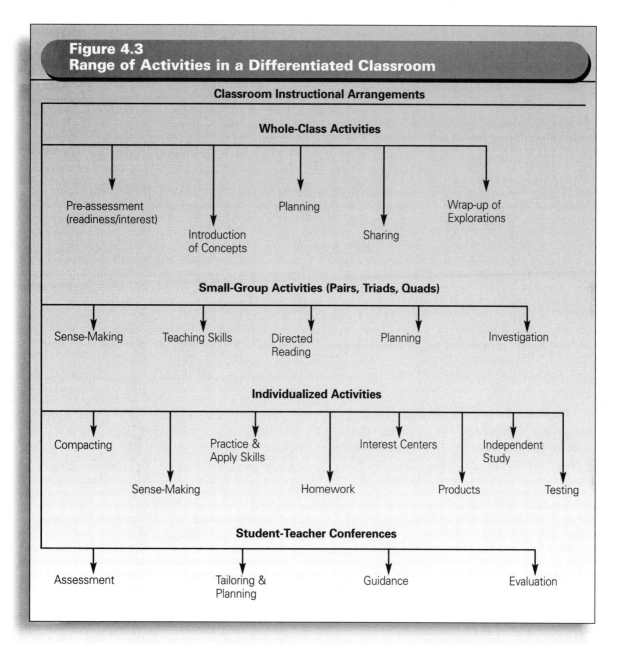

Figure 4.3
Range of Activities in a Differentiated Classroom

Classroom Instructional Arrangements

Whole-Class Activities

Pre-assessment (readiness/interest)   Introduction of Concepts   Planning   Sharing   Wrap-up of Explorations

Small-Group Activities (Pairs, Triads, Quads)

Sense-Making   Teaching Skills   Directed Reading   Planning   Investigation

Individualized Activities

Compacting   Sense-Making   Practice & Apply Skills   Homework   Interest Centers   Products   Independent Study   Testing

Student-Teacher Conferences

Assessment   Tailoring & Planning   Guidance   Evaluation

we get little firsthand experience with effectively functioning groups. Sometimes, the best way to know how to help students succeed in small group settings is just to study groups at work in your classroom, and try to list the traits of functional versus dysfunctional groups. Then try to create tasks and give directions that steer students toward the more functional ways of working. Remember that students can and should help you develop groups that are productive if you will involve them in goal setting, reflection, and problem solving. Figure 4.2 provides a few guidelines for establishing productive groups. Figure 4.3 shows a range of grouping activities.

In general, remember that groups will work better if students know what to do, how to do it, what is expected of group members, and what will constitute quality of both working processes and product. Also reflect on the fact that an effective task will call for a meaningful contribution from every group member. That is not likely to occur when some members of the group have all the answers and skills and others clearly have a comparative deficit in knowledge and skills. Groups should not establish a caste system whereby some students in the class are always the teachers and others are always the taught. Also remember to have a respectful "way out" of the group for a student who cannot, at the moment, succeed with the group, even with your assistance and the assistance of the group. The alternative should not be punitive, but should rather present a different work setting that is more likely to succeed at the time.

•**Plan with flexible grouping in mind.** In a differentiated classroom, you will often design tasks for students based on your best judgment of their readiness for and interest in those tasks, as well as how they learn best. At such times, you will most likely want to assign students to the appropriate task. At other times, you may want students to quickly discuss an idea with a nearby or pre-assigned thinking partner. Or it may be more convenient to have students work with others at their table or to turn desks into a circle with four students in a cluster. Often, students can select their task partners, or they may need or prefer to work alone.

Using a variety of grouping strategies allows you to match students and tasks when necessary, and to observe and assess students in a variety of groupings and task conditions. This flexibility also keeps students from feeling that they are "pegged" into a given classroom niche. During the course of a unit, there will be times when it makes most sense for students of a similar readiness level to work together or with the teachers. There should be other times when tasks are designed to bring together students of differing readiness levels in a way that will be meaningful to them all. There will be times when students with similar interests should work together on an area they all care about— and times when students with different specialties can come together to look at an idea or topic from several different angles.

Figure 4.3 suggests that teachers in a differentiated classroom plan for flexible grouping at the outset of a unit, asking, for example: When during the unit should the class work as a whole? When should I plan small group activities? When does it make most sense for students to work individually? When should I plan time to meet with individuals? Flexible grouping is a central part of respect for all learners, honoring individual differences, collaboration, teaching for success, and collaboration in a differentiated classroom.

❦ ❦ ❦

The next chapter offers several scenarios of how teachers of different grades and subjects have used these guidelines to transform their role in the classroom.

A Look Inside SOME Differentiated CLASSROOMS

There is no recipe for differentiation. Teachers construct differentiated classrooms in varying ways depending on their own personalities, the nature of the subject and grade level they teach, and the learning profiles of their students. These teachers have at least two things in common, however: a conviction that students differ in their learning needs, and a belief that classrooms in which students are active learners, decision makers, and problem solvers are more natural and effective than those in which students are passive recipients of information.

Although there is no formula for differentiation, taking a glimpse at some differentiated classrooms is often helpful in envisioning how differentiation can be applied. The following "tour" includes modes of differentiation appropriate for all grade levels and subjects.

Ms. Eames and Her 1st Graders

It's early spring, and Ms. Eames's 1st graders are sporting a wide range of reading levels as well as burgeoning interests in many different topics. One way Ms. Eames addresses both differences in her learners is with a flexible reading program. Each week, she posts the reading schedule. Students find their own names on the schedule and go to the appointed part of the room at times designated on the chart. In the course of the week, students are likely to read in as many as five or six configurations. There are always times when the whole class meets to listen to a story and talk about it, or to volunteer to read parts of the story. Sometimes a small group of students meets with their teacher to work on decoding, comprehension strategies, or talking about reading just for the pleasure of sharing ideas. At other points, students meet with peers who want to read on a topic of mutual interest, regardless of their reading readiness. There may be books at different reading levels on the same topic, or students may read varying portions of the same material. Students also read alone—sometimes from discovery boxes which they can browse for books of interest on a number of topics, and sometimes from boxes of books designated with a color, and matching their reading level. Sometimes students meet with a read-aloud partner. In these instances, they may take turns reading, or the teacher may ask them to "choral read" so that a stronger reader can provide leadership for a peer who does not yet read quite as well. This sort of flexible reading arrangement enables the teacher to target particular teaching needs, provide for interest-based explorations, have students share both their skills and interests with a good range of classmates, and work with the class as a whole on reading.

(*Note:* You can find out more about some flexible approaches to reading in *Guided Reading* by Fountas & Pinnell, 1996; *Matching Books to Readers, Using Leveled Books in Guided Reading,* K-3 by Fountas & Pinnell, 1999; or *Readers' Workshop: Real Reading* by Haggerty, 1992.)

Mrs. Riley and Her 3rd Graders

Mrs. Riley uses a number of differentiation strategies, but one she finds quite natural is the use of learning centers and interest centers. Based on an assumption that all learners need exposure to the same information, she used to create centers and then send each child to every center. Now, after designing a variety of centers based on her students' learning profiles, Mrs. Riley often assigns students to centers based on her formal and informal assessment of their readiness. Even when they are assigned to a learning center, students make choices about their work in ways that address their interests and learning preferences.

Today, for example, all students will be assigned to one of two reading/writing **learning centers**. Both centers focus on themes in biographies the students have read. At each center, students can elect to work alone, with a partner, or with a group of three or four peers assigned to their center. At one center, students select a person they've read about and make an annotated time line of the person's early life, selecting events that they think were most important in shaping the person's life. Then they choose to either write a paper that explains their choices, draw a storyboard of the events, or act out the events one day during sharing time. Whatever way a student decides to express understanding, the focus must be on identifying themes in the life of the person about whom they read. At the other, more complex reading/writing center, students select one of the biographies they've read, as well as a fictional work they've read about a young person. Then they write about some real-life events they and some of their 3rd grade friends have experienced. Finally, after looking in all three works for common themes about growing up, they design a method of showing how those themes are used in each setting. Mrs. Riley gives them three suggestions: theme trees; a matrix; and conversations between or among the subject of the biography, the fictional character, and a 3rd grader.

Some students go early in the day to one of these two reading/writing centers; after that, they work with differentiated math assignments at their desks. Other students experience this combination of activities in reverse order.

Interest centers are also available to students during the week. Offered at the same time as the biography-focused learning centers, some interest centers allow students to explore the skills of acting, learn how to make storyboards for advertisements and animated films, or use a laser disc to find out more about a famous person they're interested in. Mrs. Riley also offers interest centers on science- and math-related topics. Students select which interest centers to attend. Most interest centers in Mrs. Riley's classroom are available for two weeks or more.

Mr. Blackstone and His 6th Graders

Mr. Blackstone teaches science and math to students on his middle school team. This week, the team is studying inertia. To introduce this unit, Mr. Blackstone first uses whole-class instruction to ensure that all students have a grasp of key ideas. Then, students learn more about inertia by working at one of two labs designed to help them understand, analyze, and apply important unit-related principles. One lab employs a more multifaceted, complex, and ambiguous problem than the other. The teacher assigns students to the lab he feels is most appropriate for them, based on observation of the students over time, dialogue during the whole-class introduction, and "exit cards" on which students summarized what they had learned about key principles of inertia as they left the whole-class session.

Following the labs, students take a test that assesses how well they've learned the key principles from their whole-class study and differentiated labs. Students who show mastery on the test can begin working on a rocketry project, either alone or with one or two other classmates who have also shown mastery. Students who do not yet show mastery begin working on a different rocketry project, one that is more structured and ensures they reencounter and apply the key principles. Mr. Blackstone works with this group of students, guiding their thinking so they can apply important understandings. He also works periodically with the more advanced group on their project, pushing their thinking further, and avoiding the role of "the remediator."

By working with small groups much of the time, Mr. Blackstone gets to know his students and how they think. Because Mr. Blackstone

enjoys both his subject and his students, everyone in the class looks forward to opportunities to work directly with him.

Ms. Jeffries and Her 8th Grade History Students

Ms. Jeffries is determined to help her students understand that history is alive and well, so her students often work on investigative projects that help them explore themes common to history over time and place. She has designed a project to help them explore what went on in their Virginia town during the Civil War. All students begin this project by reading material available in class, viewing videos, and doing some library research. During these activities, they note in their individual learning logs information they will use for background material. Next, they make individual selections of resources from a menu of references and other sources that Ms. Jeffries has prepared. In individual conversations, she often adds one or two additional resources to a student's list based on her assessment of that learner's interests and reading/comprehension levels, as well as her sense of topics they might enjoy. Students also have to find at least one source of information that is not in their classroom or school library (Ms. Jeffries's source list includes possibilities such as talking with teachers in the school, interviewing students who have completed the study in previous years, or going to a nearby public library or museum).

As they do their in-class or library research, Ms. Jeffries encourages students to share with one another in a round-robin discussion both sources and ideas they find interesting. Students also keep a running class list of topics that they might explore for their investigations, such as medical practice in their town during the Civil War, disease patterns, the economy, the architecture and buildings in the town then and now, roles of local citizens in the military, local politics during that period, and schooling or education during the Civil War. Within two to four days, students decide on a first and second choice for their investigation, which they submit to their teacher.

Ms. Jeffries then assigns students to groups by their topics and strengths. Sometimes she constructs mixed-ability groups of five or six students; other times, she pairs students of relatively similar ability who have common interests and work well together. This flexible grouping strategy allows her to tailor projects for advanced students or for students who need more structure and guidance.

A key principle in her class, however, is the importance of working as colleagues, so students in one group are free to call on students in any other group for advice or assistance with a specific task, such as computer work, drawing, or editing. She also pairs students across groups every few days so they can share ideas that might benefit other students doing similar investigations. The tone is one of cooperation for mutual success, not competition for scarce rewards. Ms. Jeffries negotiates with her students to determine the criteria for the content, format, and quality of final products. Some criteria apply to the class as a whole, while others are specific to a group or individual task.

Ms. Jeffries designed this project carefully: It has both clearly defined, "custom-fit" responsibilities for each student, and vague, unassigned components that each group must work out how to handle. Every student has an opportunity to make a clear, individual contribution to the whole that is personally challenging and interesting. And all students engage in tasks that help them improve their negotiating and group-work skills.

Mr. Rakes and His High School Math Students

Mr. Rakes has found that by the time students enter Algebra II, their levels of math skill are quite varied. Some students seem to grasp the principles in a chapter almost before they read it; others look squint-eyed and genuinely puzzled as their peers put homework answers on the board. Somewhere in the middle are students who grasp the ideas, but more slowly or only after repeated explanations.

When Mr. Rakes used whole-class instruction to address everyone's needs in only one way, he found that he was unsuccessful with most of his students. So he began thinking of his class differently. Now, when beginning a new chapter, he offers students a chance to "compact out" of the chapter either before the class begins working on it, or after three days of work with the entire class. "Compacting out" works like this: Prior to or early on in studying a chapter, students take the chapter post-test. Those who demonstrate competency then do an ongoing, independent investigation that explores uses of mathematics in the world. Mr. Rakes gives those students guidelines for developing the independent studies, but the students get to choose the specific exploration and design the project. Sometimes students work alone on their investigations, and sometimes in small groups. Mr. Rakes works with them to tighten or focus plans, as needed.

Students like the "compacting out" option because it gives them a chance to work with many topics that interest them, but that they seldom have a chance to examine in depth during high school—topics such as computers, astronomy, architecture, medicine, and economics. Students working on independent studies can work in class (if they don't distract others), request library time (if they use the privilege appropriately), or even do another assignment during math class to free up time for work on the independent study after school. Each student creates a time line of project tasks and is accountable for meeting deadlines and keeping a process log of project work and thought.

When the other students have completed working through the chapter, *all* students take the end-of-chapter tests. This practice assures that those who compacted out of the chapter stay fresh with the skills; it also assures Mr. Rakes that everyone understands the material. Prior to this test, Mr. Rakes often takes two days for peer review, which he does by constructing mixed-ability groups in which all students work together to complete review problems.

By the time the second semester starts, a few students who weren't advanced enough for compacting during the first semester will have progressed to the point where they can opt for compacting and the math application independent study. Sometimes, a few students who had compacted out the first semester feel more comfortable if they work along with the class during the second semester. And a few students who had compacted during the first semester will again do so during the second semester. They often design independent projects that are extensions of their earlier independent studies.

When Mr. Rakes works with the students who have not compacted out, he uses a two-part study plan. First, he uses whole-group instruction to teach key principles. Next, he creates cooperative groups so students who seem able to apply the ideas somewhat independently can practice doing so. Students who are still struggling then work directly with Mr. Rakes during the first part of each class period so that he can assess their thinking and help them focus on missing concepts and skills.

During the last portion of the class, while this group is working in pairs on application tasks, Mr. Rakes checks in with the cooperative groups that have been working without his guidance.

Mr. Rakes has found this three-part approach to his class manageable for him and productive for his students. He has also begun to encourage *all* of his students to do math application studies as a part of their individual portfolio work. Although some students' individual projects may not be as complex or time-consuming as others, the projects give all students a chance to see math in a different light and to explore their interests. Some students, for example, learn about how math is used outside the textbook and the classroom by visiting and interviewing people in their community who use math in their work.

The Teacher's Toolbox

These five teachers use a variety of instructional strategies to help them match content, process, and product to the readiness, interest, and talents of their students. Some of the strategies described were interest and learning centers, mixed-ability and matched-ability cooperative groups, working as colleagues, negotiated criteria, compacting out, independent investigations, and peer review (see the Appendix for a comprehensive and descriptive list of these and other instructional strategies that are useful for managing differentiated classrooms).

❧ ❧ ❧

The next chapter offers 17 "megastrategies" you can use to move away from one-size-fits-all instruction and toward designing instruction that challenges students individually by offering a variety of learning and working arrangements.

Strategies **FOR** Managing **A** Differentiated Classroom

For many teachers, uncertainty about how to manage a differentiated classroom grows into a fear that stops them from attempting to provide instruction based on their students' varied interests and needs. Many teachers don't appreciate how skilled they are at attending to multiple signals and juggling a variety of roles. The same skills that help teachers succeed in the complex environment of a classroom can lead them toward success in a differentiated classroom environment, as well.

Benefits for Students and Teachers

As Piaget (1969) reflected, "The heartbreaking difficulty in pedagogy, as indeed in medicine and other branches of knowledge that partake at the same time of art and science, is, in fact, that the best methods are also the most difficult ones" (p. 69). Although managing a differentiated classroom is not always easy, progress in that direction tends to make school a better fit for more students. It also tends to make teaching more satisfying and invigorating.

Managing a Differentiated Classroom: The Basics

Worthwhile endeavors are often challenging— and usually worth it. Here are 17 key strategies you can use to successfully meet the challenge of designing and managing differentiated instruction for your learners.

1 Have a strong rationale for differentiating instruction based on student readiness, interest, and learning profile. Then share your thinking with your students and their parents—often. Just as teachers sometimes need help creating new mental images of classrooms as places that are fluid and offer many avenues to learning, so do students and parents.

If you help your students and parents understand and contribute to your new view of the classroom, they will be able to adapt. Without your help, they may feel that you are "violating the rules of the game," and then they may become confused or resistant. This communication strategy is so important that the next chapter more fully describes a way to prepare yourself, your students, and their parents for a student-centered, differentiated classroom.

2 **Begin differentiating at a pace that is comfortable for you.** Some teachers already make frequent adjustments in curriculum and instruction to allow for student differences in their classrooms. With just a few additional guidelines, these teachers are ready to move ahead quickly in differentiating instruction. Others who are less experienced or confident need to move in smaller increments. There's a strong parallel to students in a classroom here: Some leap like leopards through a given task, others move at a more measured gait. What matters most is that students—and teachers—make progress from their respective beginning points, not that they all work alike.

You may easily envision yourself working with varied learning resources, such as differing texts, multilevel supplementary materials, various computer programs, or peer tutors. You may, on the other hand, feel more comfortable using a single text with your class but allowing some students to move through it more rapidly, or differentiating activities so students gain—at their own pace—an understanding of ideas in the text. Perhaps you'd find it easiest to differentiate student products. Creating small-group tasks tailored to student readiness, interest, or talent may be more your style. Or you may want to begin by learning to use groups in your class—not varying the group tasks at first, but just gaining skill and confidence in directing groups. If you teach multiple subjects, you may want to try your hand first in the subject you

enjoy most. If you teach different groups of students each day, you might find it advantageous to begin differentiating instruction for the group you find easiest to work with. Finding your point of readiness and beginning there is as important for you as for your students. Not beginning is a guaranteed way to avoid progress. Biting off too much invites discouragement and failure. Begin where you can and chart a time line for your own progress. Figure 6.1 (see next page) lists some approaches to differentiation that tend to take less preparation time from teachers—and others that are likely to require more preparation time. One approach to becoming comfortable with differentiation in a way that doesn't overtake your life is to select a few low-prep strategies you're comfortable using consistently during a year, and then selecting one high prep approach per unit or semester to add to your repertoire. During a second year, you can hone the low and high prep approaches from the previous year, and add one or two more high and low prep approaches. In that cumulative way, you can work your way to a highly differentiated classroom in four or five years, without feeling absolutely frenzied along the way.

3 **Time differentiated activities to support student success.** Some students can manage group or independent work for long periods of time. Others have less capacity to sustain group or independent tasks. When designing your tasks, remember two things: (1) time allotted for a task should be a bit shorter than the attention span of the students who work on that task, and (2) advanced learners often have extended attention spans. When designing tasks for students with strong interest and ability in a particular area, allow a longer chunk of time during a class, day, or week than the amount of time planned for tasks for students whose interest or talent in the same area is not as great. A goal to strive for, over time, is helping all

**Figure 6.1
Begin Slowly—Just Begin!**

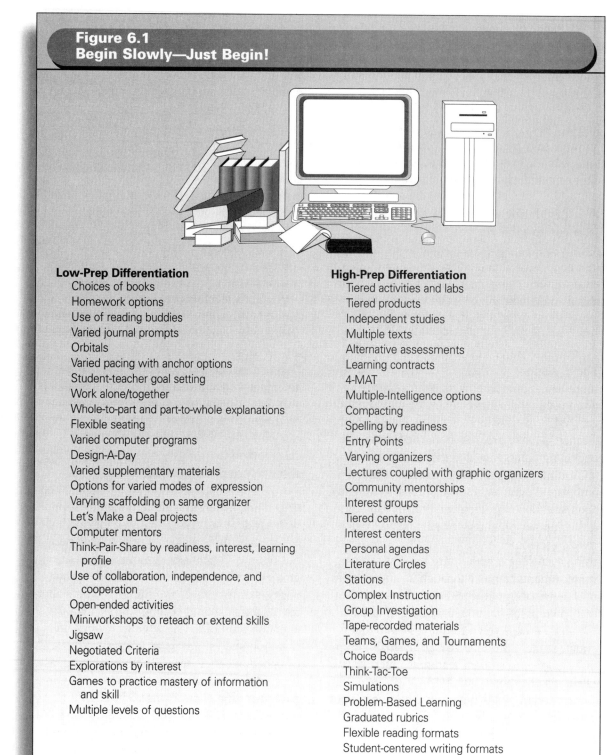

Low-Prep Differentiation
- Choices of books
- Homework options
- Use of reading buddies
- Varied journal prompts
- Orbitals
- Varied pacing with anchor options
- Student-teacher goal setting
- Work alone/together
- Whole-to-part and part-to-whole explanations
- Flexible seating
- Varied computer programs
- Design-A-Day
- Varied supplementary materials
- Options for varied modes of expression
- Varying scaffolding on same organizer
- Let's Make a Deal projects
- Computer mentors
- Think-Pair-Share by readiness, interest, learning profile
- Use of collaboration, independence, and cooperation
- Open-ended activities
- Miniworkshops to reteach or extend skills
- Jigsaw
- Negotiated Criteria
- Explorations by interest
- Games to practice mastery of information and skill
- Multiple levels of questions

High-Prep Differentiation
- Tiered activities and labs
- Tiered products
- Independent studies
- Multiple texts
- Alternative assessments
- Learning contracts
- 4-MAT
- Multiple-Intelligence options
- Compacting
- Spelling by readiness
- Entry Points
- Varying organizers
- Lectures coupled with graphic organizers
- Community mentorships
- Interest groups
- Tiered centers
- Interest centers
- Personal agendas
- Literature Circles
- Stations
- Complex Instruction
- Group Investigation
- Tape-recorded materials
- Teams, Games, and Tournaments
- Choice Boards
- Think-Tac-Toe
- Simulations
- Problem-Based Learning
- Graduated rubrics
- Flexible reading formats
- Student-centered writing formats

students sustain group and independent tasks- for longer than what was initially comfortable for them. The key to reaching that goal is their sense of success in those tasks.

4 Use an "anchor activity" to free you up to focus your attention on your students. "Ragged time" is a reality in a differentiated classroom. It is not your goal to have everyone finish all tasks at the same time, so some students will inevitably complete work while others have more to do. Using specified activities to which students automatically move when they complete an assigned task is important both to maintaining a productive work environment and to ensuring wise use of everyone's time. In almost every classroom, all students, from time to time, engage in activities like reading, journal writing, managing a portfolio, and practicing (spelling, computation, learning math through using tubs of manipulatives, and vocabulary). These sorts of tasks can become "anchor activities" that are options for students after assigned work is completed at a high level of quality. Begin by teaching your whole class to work independently and quietly on these tasks. Then move toward having half of the class work on the anchor activity (which can be adjusted to student readiness and interest), while the other half engages in a different content-based activity designed specifically for their needs. This may help you feel less fragmented in the beginning, because a sizable portion of the class will be engaged in work that is largely self-directed, freeing you to guide students in the newer and "less predictable" task. Later on, you can flip-flop the class, having the group that first worked with the anchor activity switch to an appropriate content-based activity, and vice versa. Then, when you feel ready, you can have a third of the class working with an anchor activity and two-thirds working with two differentiated content-based tasks. All sorts of combinations are possible. Do whatever feels

best to phase you and your students into an environment where multiple avenues to learning are the norm. Ultimately, your aim is to have all students understand that when they complete a given assignment, they must automatically move to an anchor activity and work with that activity with care and concentration.

5 Create and deliver instructions carefully. Giving multiple directions to the class as a whole is confusing and calls too much attention to who is doing what. A better alternative is creating and giving task cards or assignment sheets to individuals or groups. Another option is going over an assignment with a few responsible students today so that they can share directions with their groups tomorrow. It is also helpful to tape-record directions, especially when they are complex, so students can replay them as needed. Tape-recorded directions are also handy for students with reading or sequencing problems. Be sure you've thought through directions carefully, have anticipated student problems, and have struck a balance between clarity and challenge. When part of the directions require students to move to another place in the classroom, specify a time limit for the movement to be complete (shorter is generally better than longer—but not so short that it causes students to dash) with clear expectations for what constitutes orderly movement.

6 Assign students into groups or seating areas smoothly. It's bulky and confusing to call students' names in order to send them to various seating areas or to assign them to particular groups. You'll find it's smoother to list names by color or group on an overhead transparency that also indicates where the colors or groups should report. Wall charts work well also, especially for groups that will have a somewhat extended duration. For young students, peg-boards and key tags with students' names on them allow you to "move" students to a learning center or section of the room flexibly and with ease.

7 Have a "home base" for students. Beginning and ending a class or lesson from a "home base" or seating chart enables you to organize students and materials more effectively when there will be student movement during the class or lesson. In middle and high school classes, assigned or home base seats also allow you to check attendance without "calling the roll."

8 Be sure students have a plan for getting help when you're busy with another student or group. You can help students learn to work collegially by suggesting that they ask a peer for clarification when they get "stuck." Some classrooms have an "expert of the day" desk where one or more students especially skilled with the day's task sit and serve as consultants. (Astute teachers ensure that many students serve as "experts"; students also assist by checking answers, proofreading, answering questions about directions or texts, and helping with art or construction tasks.) Or students may try to get themselves "unstuck" by "thinking on paper" in their learning logs. Be sure students know when it's okay to come to you for help— and when it's not—and that they know and use several options if they need help when you are unavailable. For you to successfully manage a differentiated classroom, your students must know that it's never okay for them to just sit and wait for help to come to them, or to disrupt someone else.

9 Minimize noise. When students are active in a classroom, there will be some noise. There is no need for the noise to become oppressive or distracting. From the beginning of the year, work with students on working with peers quietly. Teach them to whisper or talk softly. Use a signal (such as turning the light on and off quickly) to remind them to reduce the conversation level. Assign a student in each group to monitor the noise level and remind peers to talk softly. Some students are especially distracted by noise. Finding a section of the room somewhat removed from the noise may be helpful for them. If that is not adequate, using a plastic headset with ear cuffs (common items in rooms with listening stations) can be a help. Ear-plugs such as those used on airplanes can make a difference as well. Remember to involve students in conversation about balancing their needs for conversation and concentration, and let them help you find other ways to retain both.

10 Make a plan for students to turn in work. There are times in a differentiated class when multiple tasks are going on at once, and when various students may turn in several different assignments in a relatively short time span. It is distracting for each student to come to you with the finished piece. Two strategies can eliminate the distraction. First, use an "expert of the day" who can check over a piece of work a student believes she has finished to see if it is both complete and of good quality. If the "expert" concurs that the work is ready to be turned in, have the "expert" sign the paper and have the student place it in a box or file labeled with the name of the task or an appropriate icon in a predesignated place in the room. If the "expert" feels the work is incomplete or lacking in quality, the student must continue working on the piece.

11 Teach students to rearrange the furniture. You can draw three or four floor plans with furniture arranged differently in each one and teach the students how to move the furniture quickly and quietly to correspond with the floor plan you designate (by name, number, or color). That makes you feel freer to be flexible with room arrangements than if you personally must move all the furniture each time it's rearranged. Be clear about your expectations for orderly movement, and also help students understand how the variety from their work will contribute to their classwork.

12 Minimize "stray" movement. Kids need to move around, regardless of their age. It's not necessarily a goal to keep everyone glued to her chair. On the other hand, an undue amount of idle roaming isn't likely to come to a good end either. Think through the amount of movement you will be comfortable with, and let your students know what they can and can't do. For example, it may be fine to go to an "expert of the day" if you're stuck on a math problem—but only as long as there is only one person at a time with the expert. Or, it may be that you want to designate a "gopher" for each work group who will get materials needed for the day's work, noting that only the gopher should be up from the table—and perhaps that only one group's gopher can be up at any one time. The directions need to apply as much structure as is needed to keep you and the students feeling productive—but no more structure than is necessary.

13 Promote on-task behavior. Help your students understand that you value on-task behavior because it helps them do better, helps you concentrate on what you need to do to help them, and eliminates distractions for others. Be sure to clarify what you mean by on-task behavior. If your standards are different, students may feel they are working just fine when you think otherwise. You may want to let students know that you will be giving them a daily check on how well they are using their time. You can make a list of students who are working with extra concentration and put a plus by their names. Similarly, you can make a list of students who find it very difficult to stay on task, even after coaching from you and

reminders from peers, and put a minus beside those names. Most students most days will do fine. Later, you can fill the pluses and minuses into a gradebook or daily worksheet, then add checks by everyone else's name. Most days, there will be mostly checks. Letting your students look at their pattern over a period of a week or month can help them see how you're assessing their concentration. Also importantly, seeing patterns in the students' concentration provides good assessment information for you. It may indicate a student who is frustrated because work is too hard or too easy, a student who needs a different seating arrangement, or a student who is really taking off with their work.

14 Have a plan for "quick finishers." Students who consistently complete their work early, and do so with competence, are providing a diagnosis of tasks that are insufficiently challenging. (Some bright students will lollygag so you don't notice the work is easy. That's safer than signaling a need for something more complex.) Sometimes, however, the task is right for the student, but their goal is simply to be the first one finished. In instances like this, it's important for the student to know that you understand their competence, but that what you're interested in is "knock your socks off" quality. Ask them to tell you several indicators or characteristics of superior thought and craftsmanship on the piece of work. Feel free to contribute some indicators yourself. Don't accept work that doesn't bear those hallmarks.

15 Make a plan for "calling a halt." While you will want to use time flexibly in a differentiated classroom, the time will come when you simply need to bring closure to a lesson sequence or unit. There may still be students not yet finished. It's important to think through how you will handle that. Some helpful approaches include: giving students advance warning (a day or two ahead of time, for example) of when the deadline will be, providing alternative homework assignments so students who want to can have a night or two to finish the work at home, using a learning contract or anchor activity time to allow for some additional work, or letting the student help you figure out how he can complete unfinished work, even as the class moves on.

16 **Give your students as much responsibility for their learning as possible.** Not only does fostering student responsibility make classroom management far more effective, it also helps young learners become independent—an important learning goal on its own. Students can pass out folders and other materials, critique one another's work, move furniture for group work, keep records of their own work, chart their progress by using established goals, help design some of their own tasks, and make suggestions for smoother classroom operation. We often underestimate the capacity of students to be self-sufficient.

17 **Engage your students in talking about classroom procedures and group processes.** Your "metacognition," or thinking aloud about your thinking, helps students understand your expectations as well as rationales for those expectations. It also helps them develop ownership in their classroom. Having ongoing conversations about what you're all experiencing individually and collectively is a great investment in the future—saving much more time and stress in the long run than these conversations require at the time. Besides, you'll be amazed at how many times the students can spot and think of a solution to a problem before you can figure it out. Use their eyes and minds to make the class work smoothly and comfortably.

🐾 🐾 🐾

There are many other effective ways to develop a classroom in which students engage in a variety of interesting and engaging activities. Share your management-of-differentiation strategies with colleagues and ask them to share with you what works for them.

Preparing Students **AND** Parents **FOR A** Differentiated Classroom

In a differentiated classroom, some of the traditional ground rules change. Your students and their parents may initially need your help to understand and feel comfortable with the new look and feel of the classroom. After an initial period of uncertainty, most students and parents respond quite positively to a setting that treats individuals as unique people and where learning is active and engaging. This chapter offers some strategies for making students and parents feel "at home" in a differentiated classroom.

Introducing Students to Differentiated Instruction: A Middle School Scenario

Mrs. Middleton begins the school year with a clear idea of how she wants her differentiated middle school English classes to work. Knowing she needs her students' help to reach that goal,

she has developed an effective way both to orient her students to the environment she wants to create for them and to enlist their help in creating it.

First, Mrs. Middleton shows her students how to make a line graph. Students choose ways to describe the quality of something, which they then position as labels along the vertical axis. Each class chooses different descriptors, but the top (best) labels are often "awesome" or "way cool" or "in orbit." The bottom (worst) labels tend to be "disaster zone" or "dismal" or "dead meat." Students also label several points in between the best and worst indicators. Next, Mrs. Middleton asks the students to put descriptors along the horizontal axis, such as "good in writing," "good in math," "good in soccer," "good in reading," "good in cleaning my room," "good in spelling." Then she asks them to add four or five descriptors of their own choosing. To help her students understand how to plot themselves on their graph, she makes a graph of herself on the board while the students watch. She plots herself as very strong with writing, somewhat strong with math, weaker with spelling, about average with soccer and cleaning her room, and so on. When she plots herself on each of her additional descriptors—"good with photography," "good with cartooning," and "good with crossword puzzles"—she discusses her interest in each area. Students complete their graph for homework, and each day for the next couple of weeks, three or four students share their graph with the class. Then Mrs. Middleton's students tape their graphs, grouped by class period, on an empty classroom wall.

After a few days, Mrs. Middleton asks her students what patterns they see in the graphs, and she lists the ones they note. Students usually see several patterns quickly, especially the first two in the following list:

- Everybody said they are better in some things and worse in others.
- Nobody drew a flat line and said they were the same in everything.
- More girls than boys said they were good spellers.
- More kids in 5th period said they were good writers.
- People mostly added things they were good at.

Mrs. Middleton takes a minute to reflect on their responses, and then she poses this question to her students: "If you are different in your strengths—even in English (some of you said you were strong in spelling and weak in reading, for example)—what should I do about that?"

Her students' response to this question is usually that she should deal with them in different ways based on their differences. They often suggest that her main goal should be to help them all grow, both in their strengths and in their weaker areas. Sometimes they say that this means they should not all do the same tasks all the time in class. Some older classes have even offered her specific examples, such as giving advanced spelling assignments to students who are great spellers, or less difficult writing assignments if writing is very hard for some students.

Then, over several days, Mrs. Middleton engages her students in discussions about how their class has to function if different things are going on in a single class period, and they help her establish rules for a class like that. They even discuss grading and decide that students should be graded on their individual progress, not in comparison to everyone else. The students talk about ways to set individual goals with the teacher, keep track of their own work and progress, and help one another succeed.

Mrs. Middleton concludes this "preparation" phase by summarizing what they've all agreed is necessary and putting a summary of their ideas on chart paper in front of the room. "In this classroom," she says, "'fair' will mean that all of us must live by the class rules, all of us must work hard, all of us must respect one another and encourage one another. It does not mean we'll all do the same things all the time." She lets her students know it is okay to come to her and say they'd really like to be working with a particular topic or project someone else is doing. "Lots of times," she assures them, "I'll be able to let you know when that will come up for you, because I'll make sure that all of you get your share of both the 'good stuff' and the 'drudge work.'"

Gradually, students begin practicing the procedures for distributing work folders, free reading, individual conferences with the teacher, individualized spelling, small-group projects, writing critique groups, and so on. Each day, Mrs. Middleton takes some time for metacognition: She asks her students to briefly assess how they did as individuals and as a group toward achieving their operational goals and following their new ground rules.

Mrs. Middleton helps her students understand that some days she assigns them to tasks and work groups, and that some days they get to select for themselves. She also makes certain to use all sorts of grouping arrangements. She made a critical discovery about her grouping strategies one day simply by overhearing a student say to a friend, "I think Mrs. Middleton stays up nights trying to figure out another way to scramble us up." Mrs. Middleton learned not only to give her students more insight into her grouping strategies, but also to ask her students to be active partners with her in figuring out how their work is going for them.

Now she remembers to say from time to time, "Let me know if you think what you're doing is too hard or too easy for you, and I'll take a look at it with you. We can make changes when we need to."

Another way she gives her students opportunities to be active partners with her is to occasionally allow them to design minicontracts in which they work with an interesting activity they've seen or to extend something they especially enjoyed doing.

In school—just like everywhere else—there's probably no such thing as a perfect day, but Mrs. Middleton and her students have lots of very good days, and few really rough days. Mrs. Middleton's classroom is a comfortable, busy, and respectful place, one that both teacher and students work to successfully create.

Introducing Students and Parents to Differentiation: A Primary Grade Scenario

Mr. Wade sends a survey home to parents early in the year, asking parents to provide the approximate ages of their children when they began to do things like walking, talking, singing, riding a tricycle, dressing themselves, and so on. He charts the results and, not surprisingly, always finds that in every endeavor,

some students accomplished the task well before others. To the students in class, he raises the question, "Does it seem to matter much that somebody began talking nearly a year before someone else? Seems like everyone in here is talking fine now!" The students agree that when they began to talk is not nearly so important as that they did begin to talk. Mr. Wade uses that as a reminder in class that some students will learn to count higher and faster or read more comfortably sooner. That's fine, the students agree, as long as everyone is working on the skills they need.

With parents at parents' night Mr. Wade also adds a conversation about what would have happened had they forced a child to walk before he could stand, or run before he could walk, or if they had spent every day in a hovering panic because the child next door was talking and their child was not. He helps the parents realize that school is a progression of life and that teaching is like parenting in some ways. He can discover where the child is in a sequence of skills, provide opportunities for next steps, encourage and ensure affirmation for progress. He cannot force them to match the kid at the next table. Nor, he points out, should he silence the student who is already talking until the other students find their voice. The analogy helps parents throughout the year understand Mr. Wade's thinking when he differentiates instruction. He invites parents to help him understand their child's development and interests so that together they can be effective catalysts for growth.

Helping Parents Learn About Differentiated Instruction

Most parents are eager for their students to learn, grow, succeed, and feel accepted in school. A differentiated classroom is an ideal place for those things to take place. You share those goals with your students' parents. It's just the way a differentiated classroom "looks" that's different from what parents may expect. You can help them develop a clear, positive understanding of differentiated instruction and how it benefits their children. Let them know that:

• The goal of differentiated instruction is to make certain that everyone grows in all key skills and knowledge areas, moving on from their starting points.

• In a differentiated classroom, the teacher closely assesses and monitors skills, knowledge levels, interests, and effective ways of learning for all students, and then plans lessons and tasks with those levels in mind.

• A differentiated lesson assigned by a teacher reflects the teacher's current best understanding of what a child needs to grow in understanding and skill. That understanding is evolutionary and will change as the year goes on, as the child grows, and as parents contribute to the understanding.

• The teacher will be glad to have parents come to school and talk about their children because both have important perspectives to share. A teacher sees a student more broadly in regard to agemates and developmental benchmarks. A parent sees a student more deeply in regard to interests, feelings, and change over time. When the wide-angle lens and close-up lens both add images of the child, the picture becomes fuller for everyone.

• A goal in your classroom is to help each student become a more independent learner.

A Note About Differentiation and Parents of Advanced Learners

Parents of advanced learners often get labeled as pushy. No doubt some of them are (as are some parents of any group of learners). For the most part, however, they want the right things for the children. They value learning, want their chil-dren to do the same, and are eager for a class-room that challenges and invigorates their students. Many of these parents have come to distrust school because their children have spent so many years in school waiting for others to learn what they already knew. There are several important points to consider when working with parents of highly able students (many apply to most parents).

• **Listen to them and learn from them.** They have a story to tell and want someone to hear it and to be invested in the growth of their child. All parents ought to get that kind of reception in school.

• **Rebuild their trust that school is a good fit for their child.** As they see your investment in tapping into and extending their child's understandings, skills, talents, and interests, you are likely to see skepticism replaced by gratitude.

• **Understand the paradox of parenting a bright child.** Most parents of highly able students want their child challenged. They know that a good piano teacher recognizes musical talent and mentors the student in developing that talent. Most of them recognize that a coach recognizes athletic talent and pushes the young person to extend that capacity. On the one hand, parents of bright learners want that sort of challenge in their child's classrooms. On the other hand, however, they, like their children, may have become addicted to success.

Further, they are parents and don't like to see their child struggle. So, while they want a challenge for their child, they may also want you to guarantee that the challenge will involve no risk, no stumbling, no failure. Those two desires are incompatible. Risk-free talent development, painless challenge, and growth without tension are anomalies, if they exist at all.

You may have to help some parents realize that. Then, your message ought to be, "I see the potential in your child. I am excited about being a part of developing that potential. I can't do that and promise that everything will be easy for him. I can't promise that As will remain automatic. I can promise you, however, that I am aware of the struggle and will do everything I can to be a partner with your child in learning to struggle, overcoming obstacles, and ultimately discovering that he has a far greater capacity than he thought he did. My goal is not to punish him or to cause him to fail in the long term. To the contrary, I know I will be an effective teacher if I can help him learn to rise to a challenge, to find satisfaction in effort. Will you help me with that?"

•**Think through the "Why is her work harder" question**. If you establish the sort of understanding with parents described in the previous suggestion, you will eliminate many a tense discussion that occurs when a parent is afraid of challenge for their child (even as they seek it). Nonetheless, a parent may ask you why the work their child is doing is "harder" than that of another child in the class.

In a differentiated classroom, a readiness-based assignment needs to be just a little too hard for a student's current proficiency level. The goal of the teacher is to ensure, as often as possible, that each student has to work a little too hard, and to find a support system that leads to success and growth.

The only answer for a parent who asks, "Why does my child have to do harder work than someone else?" is that, relative to her skills and understanding, the work is no harder for her than the work of any other child relative to that child's skills and understanding. Much of the discussion must go back to the reality that talent development takes struggle—for all humans, even very bright ones. Most students encounter struggle regularly in school. Bright

kids have to learn to do battle with it, too, if they are to become what they can be.

The noted children's author Katherine Paterson keeps a reminder above the desk where she writes, "Before the gates of excellence, the high gods have placed sweat" (1981, p. 3). Much as we might wish otherwise, we have no reason to believe she's wrong.

A Note About Parents Who Push Students Too Hard

Probably less common than the parent of bright students who want challenge and ease simultaneously are the parents who push their child to do work that is far too taxing. Here, too, it helps for a teacher to have reflected on that scenario. There is the possibility, of course, that the parent sees capability in the student that is there, but hidden from view in school. For that reason, it's not a bad idea to let a student try something you believe may be too demanding.

In the life of every teacher some of the most compelling stories are of students who bloomed when the teacher had no expectation of it. On the other hand, there is a difference between expecting much of a child and expecting too much. If the task does appear to be too great for the child, if it causes the child tension and frustration, and if it leads to confusion and self-doubt rather than clarity and self-confidence—it's important to then help the parent understand that learning is impaired when students feel overtaxed, afraid, and out of control. A conversation something like the one described before between Mr. Wade and parents of his students might be helpful.

It is also useful if you can help the student find a voice to express his tension and unhappiness. The message may be clearer from a student than from a teacher. Also, in a setting where parents are unduly controlling, a young person often feels mute. Regaining a voice and becoming a self-advocate can be important in helping the student have a sense of power of his or her own world.

A Note About Parents Who Stay Away from School

There are many reasons why parents stay away from school. In some cases, parental absence may not create a problem. In some cases, however, the parents who stay away are ones we need most to invite into the child's world at school. Some of these parents stay away because school was alienating for them and returning is too difficult. Some stay away because they do not speak the language spoken in parent conferences. Some stay away because their lives are too burdened to add one more thing. We err as teachers in assuming that these parents don't care about their children's education. That is rare indeed.

Most parents, including those who keep their distance from us, care deeply about their children's schooling and see it as a way to achieve a good life. It is critical that schools and teachers build bridges to these parents, communicating with them in whatever ways we can find—including, but not limited to, making school a more inviting place for them. They need to hear our messages—and see concrete evidence—that we believe in their children.

They need to hear the success stories of their children. They need to receive concrete suggestions of things they can do to be partners in their children's learning.

We also need to hear from them. We need to understand better the child's culture and language and history and dreams. We need to know the stories that get brought home from school, and the parent's perspective on what will work best in helping their children learn. It is easy for us to assume that everyone's view of the world is like the one we grew up with. That is not the case. Reaching out to every parent in effective ways helps us expand our worldview—and become more effective teachers.

Successful partnering between teacher and parents is based on proactive communication. Send home information bulletins or newsletters from time to time, telling about goals for specific projects, how various procedures are working in class, and so on. Ask for parents' reactions and suggestions related to differentiation. Build partnerships with parents, just as you do with your students, to create a classroom in which individuals are honored and much is expected from every student.

❦ ❦ ❦

The next chapter begins our detailed "how to's"—this time, by focusing on students' readiness levels.

THE How To's OF Planning Lessons Differentiated by Readiness

Three characteristics of students guide differentiation: readiness, interest, and learning profile. We know that students learn better if tasks are a close match for their skills and understanding of a topic (readiness), if tasks ignite curiosity or passion in a student (interest), and if the assignment encourages students to work in a preferred manner (learning profile). In this chapter and the next two, we'll take a look at the basics of differentiating instruction in response to those three student traits. This chapter focuses on readiness differentiation. A task that's a good match for student readiness extends that student's knowledge, understanding, and skills a bit beyond what the student can do independently. A good readiness match pushes the student a little beyond his or her comfort zone and then provides support in bridging the gap between the known and unknown.

Expert teachers often do the equivalent of "playing by ear" when they differentiate instruction in their classrooms based on the readiness levels of their students. That is, they simply do what seems right for their students. Generally, intuition begins the process, and over time teachers learn from their successes and failures, refining what they do as they go along. Thus when we ask teachers how they plan a differentiated lesson in response to student readiness, their answers are often a bit vague: "I just try to match the tasks to the students' readiness level," or "I put them in groups I think will work." Clarity about differentiation by readiness can hone and refine good instincts, giving the teacher a greater sense of comfort with readiness differentiation and providing students more appropriate learning experiences.

Thinking About Differentiation by Readiness

To differentiate instruction according to student readiness successfully, it helps to have a comprehensive guide for planning and monitoring the effectiveness of differentiated curriculum. One way to get specific guidance about what teachers do when they create differentiated lessons is to study those lessons and discover what makes them differentiated. We can also learn much by asking "What supports the instinct to differentiate instruction?" Figure 8.1 is an answer to that question, derived from looking at many examples of differentiation. The tool in this figure is called "the equalizer."

Designing differentiated instruction is similar to using the equalizer buttons on a stereo or CD player. You can slide the buttons across several different continuums to get the best combination of sounds for each musical piece. In a differentiated classroom, adjusting the "buttons" appropriately for various students' needs equalizes their chances of being appropriately challenged by the materials, activities, and products in your classroom, as follows:

• **Foundational to Transformational.** When an idea is new to some students, or if it's not in one of their stronger areas, they often need supporting information about the idea that is clear and plainly worded. Then they usually need time to practice applying the idea in a straightforward way. In these instances, the materials they use and the tasks they do should be foundational—that is, basic and presented in ways that help them build a solid foundation of understanding. At other times, when something is already clear to them or is in a strength area, they need to move along quickly. They need information that shows them intricacies about the idea. They need to stretch and bend the idea and see how it interacts with other ideas to create a new thought. Such conditions require materials and tasks that are more transformational.

For example, one child may benefit from a more basic task of classifying animals by body covering, while another may need the more transformational task of predicting how changes in environment would likely affect the body covering of several animals. In a math class, one young learner may be ready for a basic application of the concept of fractions by cutting fruit and placing it to reflect a given fraction. An appropriate challenge for another student may be the more transformational task of writing measures of music that represent certain fractions.

• **Concrete to Abstract.** Students usually need to become familiar with the key information or material about an area of study before they can successfully look at its implications, meanings, or interrelationships. However, once they have grasped the information in a concrete way, it's important that they move on to meanings and implications. Working with concrete information should open a door for meaningful abstraction later on. For example, grasping the idea of plot (more concrete) typically has to precede investigations of theme (more abstract). But ultimately, all students need to delve into the meanings of stories, not just the events. The issue here is readiness or timing.

• **Simple to Complex.** Sometimes students need to see only the big picture of a topic or area of study, just its "skeleton," without many details. Even adults often find it helpful to read a children's book on black holes, for example, before they tackle the work of Stephen Hawking. When the big picture is needed, your students need resources, research, issues, problems, skills, and goals that help them achieve a framework of understanding with clarity. On the other hand, when the "skeleton" is clear to them, they'll find it more stimulating to add "muscle, bone, and nerves," moving from simple to complex. Some students may need to work more simply with one abstraction at a time; others may be able to handle the complexity of multiple abstractions.

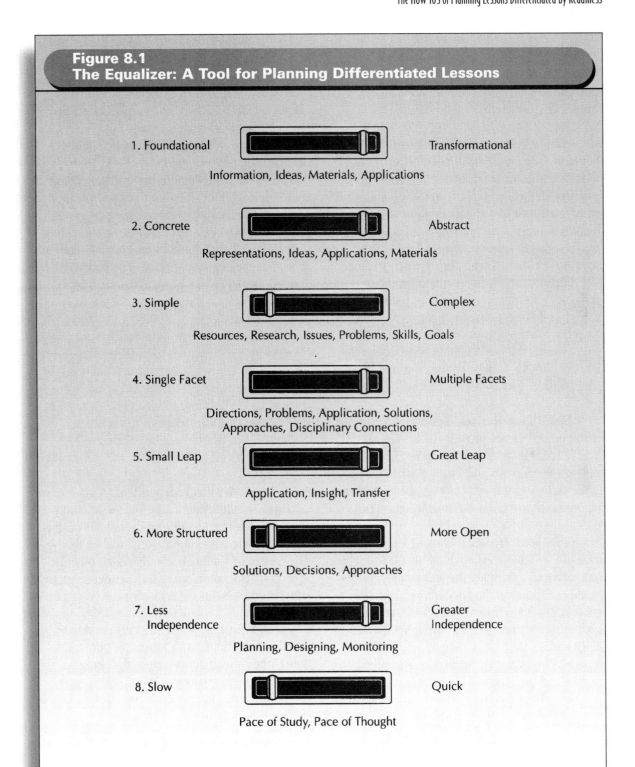

Figure 8.1
The Equalizer: A Tool for Planning Differentiated Lessons

1. Foundational — Transformational
Information, Ideas, Materials, Applications

2. Concrete — Abstract
Representations, Ideas, Applications, Materials

3. Simple — Complex
Resources, Research, Issues, Problems, Skills, Goals

4. Single Facet — Multiple Facets
Directions, Problems, Application, Solutions,
Approaches, Disciplinary Connections

5. Small Leap — Great Leap
Application, Insight, Transfer

6. More Structured — More Open
Solutions, Decisions, Approaches

7. Less Independence — Greater Independence
Planning, Designing, Monitoring

8. Slow — Quick
Pace of Study, Pace of Thought

For example, some students may be ready to work with the theme in a story (a single abstraction), while other students look at inter-relationships between themes and symbols (multiple abstractions, or complexity).

• **Single Facet to Multiple Facets**. Sometimes students are at peak performance when working on problems, projects, or dilemmas that involve only a few steps or solutions to complete. It may be all that some students can handle to make a connection between what they studied in science today and what they studied last week. Those with greater understanding and facility in an area of study are ready for and more challenged by following complicated directions. They are more challenged by solving problems that are multifaceted or require great flexibility of approach, or by being asked to make connections between subjects that scarcely seemed related before.

• **Small Leap to Great Leap**. Note that this continuum does not provide the option of "no leap." Students should always have to run ideas through their minds and figure out how to use them. Activities that call only for absorption and regurgitation are generally of little long-term use.

But for some students, learning about how to measure area and then applying that learning by estimating and verifying the area of the hamster house compared to the teacher's desk may be enough of a leap of application and transfer—at least in the beginning. Other students may be able to move from estimating and verifying area to estimating materials needed for a building project and proportional cost implications of increasing the building area. In both cases, students make mental leaps from reading information on a page to using that information. The latter task calls for relatively greater leaps of application, insight, and transfer.

• **Structured to Open-Ended.** Sometimes students need to complete tasks that are fairly well laid out for them, where they don't have too many decisions to make. Novice drivers begin by managing the car on prescribed driving ranges or delineated routes. Being new to a computer or word processor often requires completing programmed and closed lessons that involve "right" answers to become knowledgeable—and comfortable—with basic operation and keyboarding before moving on to more advanced and open-ended tasks such as selecting varied uses of graphics to illustrate ideas in a formal presentation. Following a predetermined format for a writing assignment or a chemistry lab often makes more sense than improvisation.

At other times, however, students are ready to explore the computer, craft their own essays designed to address a communication need, or create a chemistry lab that demonstrates principles of their choosing. Modeling helps most of us become confident enough to eventually "wing it." But when modeling has served its purpose, it's time to branch out and get creative.

• **Dependent to Independent.** A goal for all learners is independent study, thought, and production. But just as some students gain height more quickly than others, some will be ready for greater independence earlier than others. Their needs in developing independence generally fall into one of these four stages:

1. *Skill building*, when students need to develop the ability to make simple choices, follow through with short-term tasks, and use directions appropriately.

2. *Structured independence*, when students make choices from teacher-generated options, follow prescribed time lines, and engage in self-evaluation according to preset criteria to complete longer-term and more complex tasks.

3. *Shared independence*, when students generate problems to be solved, design tasks, set time lines, and establish criteria for evaluation. The teacher helps "tighten" or focus the plans and monitors the production process.

4. *Self-guided independence*, when students plan, execute, and evaluate their own tasks, and seek help or feedback only when needed (Tomlinson, 1993).

By guiding students across this continuum at individually appropriate speeds, you and your students are less likely to become frustrated by tasks that require greater independence.

• **Slow to Fast.** Of all the continuums, this one is the most likely to require some "jumping around." There are times when students with great ability in a subject need to move quickly through familiar or minimally challenging material.

But at other times, some of those same students will need more time than others to study a topic in depth. You can adjust the speed of learning experiences for students who are struggling with key ideas by allowing them to work more slowly at first, but then letting them move quickly through tangential areas of study, thus freeing up some time for further work with the key ideas. Matching pacing to your students' needs is a critical differentiation strategy.

Like the equalizer buttons on audio equipment, it's possible for the teacher to design lessons by "moving the buttons" on this guide to different positions for the needs of varied students.

For example, some students may be able to handle a complex, abstract, multifaceted project (buttons over to the right on Figure 8.1) if you keep the "independence" button toward the left; that is, require more "check-in" dates of them than you require of more self-guided students working on that same project.

Equalizer Troubleshooting Tips

When using the heuristic guide in Figure 8.1 to modify lessons for a differentiated classroom, keep in mind three essential caveats:

1. *All students need lessons that are coherent, relevant, powerful, transferable, authentic, and meaningful.* We should not consign some students to drill and practice as the staple of their school diets and save the rich and engaging lessons for others.

2. *A curriculum that is good for students pushes them a bit beyond what they find easy or comfortable.* Our best teaching happens when we give students a genuine challenge and then help them successfully meet it. Differentiated instruction is so powerful because it offers various levels of genuine challenge. Your students' sense of self-efficacy comes from recognizing their power after accomplishing something they first thought was just "too big" for them. Design your lessons to stretch all students beyond their comfort zones in knowledge, insight, thinking, basic skills, production and presentation skills, and affective awareness.

3. *Plan to encourage your students to "work up"—that is, be ready to match students to tasks that will stretch them.* A good task for a given student is one that is just a bit too hard and through which the teacher ensures the presence of support required for success. We err most often as teachers by planning a single task that is easy enough for most students to complete. That has the effect of establishing both "middling" or low expectations for many learners and expectations still out of the reach of others. A task is challenging for a given student when it causes that student to stand on "mental tiptoes" and reach high to complete it well.

This guide for differentiating instruction gets at the heart of what many teachers do when they adapt instruction for varied learner needs—

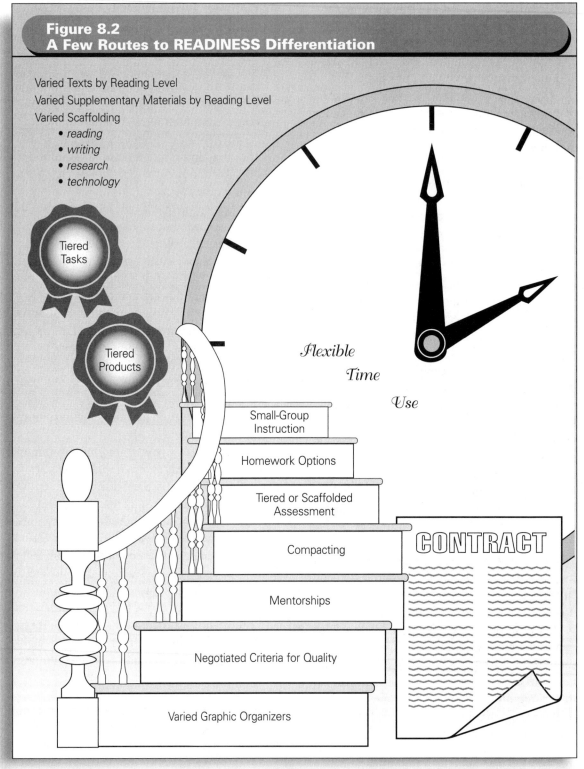

Figure 8.2
A Few Routes to READINESS Differentiation

Varied Texts by Reading Level
Varied Supplementary Materials by Reading Level
Varied Scaffolding
- *reading*
- *writing*
- *research*
- *technology*

Tiered Tasks

Tiered Products

Flexible Time Use

Small-Group Instruction

Homework Options

Tiered or Scaffolded Assessment

Compacting

Mentorships

Negotiated Criteria for Quality

Varied Graphic Organizers

CONTRACT

albeit automatically. Use this guide when differentiating content (what you teach and what students learn), process (how students think about or make sense of ideas and information), and product (how students show what they know). Add other continuums and descriptors to this guide as your students teach you more about how to differentiate instruction.

It is also helpful to think about particular strategies for differentiating instruction in response to student readiness levels. Figure 8.2 suggests a few such strategies.

In using any of the strategies to match student readiness, you are likely to be using materials, tasks, or scaffolding that corresponds to one or more continuums on the equalizer. For example, if you bookmark various Web sites for students to use in research, then try to match the difficulty level of the various sites to the skills and understanding levels of various students, you may find that some sites are more concrete and some more abstract, or that some are simpler in writing or ideas while others are more complex.

You might also have all students use the same sites, building a support system to allow success for less-skilled readers (greater dependence), while encouraging skilled readers to work more independently. Try the combination of strategies and equalizer continuums in your own classroom.

Using Readiness to Differentiate Content, Process, and Product

Teachers can differentiate any or all of the three key components of curriculum (content, process, and product) in response to student readiness. A French teacher differentiated content for her learners by subscribing to two French language current events magazines. Students who were having more difficulty with reading and translating French used a magazine written for U.S. students learning French for the first time. Students more proficient with French translation read a magazine written for French-speaking adolescents. The two magazines generally contained many articles on the same topics, but the magazine written for French-speaking adolescents required more complex skills of translation.

A math teacher often differentiated process or activities for her students based on their readiness levels by assigning or offering homework assignments on the same topic at varying degrees of difficulty. She helped students determine which assignment would be most likely to both clarify their thinking and challenge them appropriately.

A middle school teaching team differentiated product assignments based on student readiness in a number of ways. One way was using varying portions of rubrics, or quality indicators, with different students. Each student would receive two or three columns of a five-column rubric. Each student would work with the teacher to designate their goals for the product assignment. It was the aim of the teacher to provide a student with rubric columns that seemed at or above the student's proficiency level and then guide the student in "working up" through self-selected goals in each category represented on the rubric.

When teachers use readiness level as a focus for differentiating content, process, and product, their aim is to push students just a bit beyond their particular "comfort zones" so that student work is a little too hard. They then support students in stretching to achieve a next level of competency with important skills and ideas.

❦ ❦ ❦

The next chapter focuses on students' interests: how to engage students in your lessons.

THE How To's OF Planning Lessons Differentiated BY Interest

A wise teacher knows that a key feature of artful teaching is having a plan to engage or "hook" students on the topic at hand. Engagement is a nonnegotiable of teaching and learning. Two powerful and related motivators for engagement are student interest and student choice (Bess, 1997; Brandt, 1998). If a student has a spark (or better still, a fire) of curiosity about a topic, learning is more likely for that student. Similarly, a sense of choice about what or how we learn is also empowering, and thus an enhancement to learning. The trouble is, of course, that not all students in a class have the same interests, thus the need for differentiation again.

Content, process, and product can be differentiated according to student interest. One time in the year when Mr. Elkins differentiates content in response to student interest occurs during a standards-based unit on reading and writing nonfiction. While there are key under-standings and skills on which all his students will focus, he has learned that the required skills and principles are more engaging to his students when what they read and write about is of genuine interest to them. When the unit begins, he guides students in selecting reading materials and topics they care about. He then builds the unit around their selections.

Ms. Bella likes to use Jigsaw, a cooperative learning strategy, as one way of differentiating process in response to student interest. As she and her students explore a broad topic, she asks each student to select a facet of the topic that is intriguing to him or her. At some point or points in the unit, Mrs. Bella creates Jigsaw teams that ask students to specialize on the facet they selected with other students who selected the same interest area. They then share what they learn with students in another group comprised of representatives of each of the facets explored.

Mrs. Gomez finds products an ideal way to tap into student interests. She does that sometimes by offering students varied ways of expressing what they learn through their product. Sometimes she gives students elements of understanding and skill that their products must contain and then guides the students in developing their own product assignments. Often she encourages students to add their own product goals to ones she has developed for the whole class. She finds that products allow her many ways to give her students choice and voice.

There are two ways for a teacher to think about student interest. First, of course, teachers who care about their students as individuals accept the difficult task of trying to identify the interests students bring to the classroom with them. Second, dynamic teachers try to create new interests in their students. When a teacher is passionate about a topic and shares the passion with his classes, similar interests are likely to emerge in many of the learners as well.

Drawing on Existing Student Interests

Among goals of interest-based instruction are (1) helping students realize that there is a match between school and their own desires to learn, (2) demonstrating the connectedness between all learning, (3) using skills or ideas familiar to students as a bridge to ideas or skills less familiar to them, and (4) enhancing student motivation to learn. When a teacher encourages a student to look at a topic of study through the lens of that student's own interest, all four goals are likely to be achieved.

There are many strategies for drawing on student interests and linking them to the curriculum. Here are three approaches.

"Sidebar" Studies

Mrs. Janes and her students are about to begin a study on the Civil War in 7th grade history.

During the unit, she will be emphasizing concepts of culture, conflict, interdependence, and change—concepts that guide much of the year's study. As part of the unit, students will read and discuss the textbook, as well as supplementary and primary source materials. They will visit a battlefield, have speakers visit their class, and see videos on the time period. Mrs. Janes asked her students to list things they like to think and learn about in their own lives. Among topics they generated were music, sports/recreation, people, families, reading, transportation, heroes/villains, medicine, food, travel, humor, clothing, books, unsolved mysteries, cartoons, and teens.

The teacher suggested to her 7th graders that they could learn a great deal about the time period by exploring it through their own interests, as those interests were manifest during the Civil War period. She helped them set up "sidebar" investigations that would go on throughout the unit. Their job was to see what their topic showed them about life during the Civil War in general, and about culture, conflict, change, and interdependence during that time. Students could work alone or with a partner on their sidebar study.

To support student success, Mrs. Janes helped students develop planning calendars, set goals for their work, and establish criteria for quality. She set check-in dates to monitor student progress along the way, and occasionally conducted minilessons on research for students who wanted help with information finding. Sometimes students had class time to work on their sidebar investigations. When they finished daily work, they could always work with the sidebar study. Sometimes it was homework.

Mrs. Janes found that class discussions throughout the unit were punctuated with insights the students were developing through their sidebar investigations. Students had stories to tell that made the time period come alive for everyone. Motivation was high and learning was connected both to past units and to students' own lives.

Interest Centers or Interest Groups

In Mr. Nickens's primary classroom, there are always times when students can meet in interest groups. For whatever his students are studying, Mr. Nickens creates an interest center to allow his young learners to find out more about what they are curious about. For example, while students studied animal habitats, there were interest centers on habitats of varied animals such as badgers, beavers, and polar bears. In those centers, students could learn about particular habitats as a way of expanding the unit's understandings. Ultimately, students who wanted to do so could form an interest group with one or more peers to create an interest center on the habitat of another animal for their peers, as well as students next year. In interest groups, students sometimes read together, sometimes had book discussions, sometimes shared what they were finding out from their own research, planned the interest center they would design, and did the work necessary to create the interest center.

The habitat study for the whole class continued at the same time. For some students whose interests in the topic were enduring, the interest groups continued to meet on the animal and habitat they were studying well after the unit on habitats ended. The combination of interest centers and interest groups encouraged students to both develop and expand interests.

Specialty Teams

In a literature unit, Ms. Bollinger wants her 4th graders to explore ways authors use descriptive language to help readers "see" what they are writing about. Ms. Bollinger believes, however, that students will be more interested in the language exploration if she allows them to look for effective and varied examples of description in the kinds of writing they most like to read. Students will form specialty teams to look at effective description in several kinds of writing: short stories, novels, fantasy, science fiction, nature writing, poetry, lyrics, and action comics. Teams will consist of three to four students with a common interest in a particular kind of writing. Task guidelines will focus students on looking for elements central in powerful description (use of figures of speech, role of verbs and adjectives, use of slang or regional language, wordplay, words created by authors, originality, and so on). Students will need to be ready to use what they learn in their specialty teams in a class discussion. Each group will also decide on passages to nominate for the Descriptive Hall of Fame, present those passages to the class, and defend their choices. In the end, the teacher's goal of analyzing powerful description should be more dynamic and memorable by virtue of tapping student interest than if everyone read the same materials.

In each of these instances, the teacher has helped students use existing interests as a vehicle for learning more about and becoming more invested in important ideas delineated by the curriculum. In no instance did the interest-based approach detract from essential understandings and skills, but rather made them more accessible, relevant, and memorable to students with varying interests.

Expanding Student Interests

One of the great pleasures of teaching is the chance to introduce students to a world full of ideas and opportunities they've not yet discovered. Interest-based instruction can not only draw on and expand already existing student interests, but can help them discover new interests as well. Once again, there are many routes to helping students discover new interests. Here are two examples.

Real-Life Applications of Ideas and Skills

Ms. Paige is eager for her students to discover links between math and the adult world of work. Her 6th graders know little about what most adults do in their daily work—including, she has discovered, what their parents' jobs are like. She has asked each of her students to interview someone whose job seems interesting to them to find out how that person uses fractions and decimals in their occupation. Students will ask some preliminary questions to determine whether a potential interviewee does, in fact, use fractions and decimals in important ways. If not, a student will continue the search for someone whose job is of interest to the student and who does use fractions and decimals as an occupational tool. Students observe or shadow their interviewee, if possible.

Ms. Paige wants students to see that math is central to many kinds of work. She also knows that this exploration will help students develop an increased awareness of and interest in ways people earn a living and make a contribution to society. She and the students develop interview questions and develop a range of ways in which students can show what they learn. Some requirements are common to all students, including specifications for showing precisely how the person uses fractions and decimals.

Last year, students found out about the usefulness of fractions and decimals in jobs such as anesthesiology, auto repair, media specialist, secretary, pilot, pharmacist, composer, and business owner. Ms. Paige finds that math becomes "new" and exciting as students connect it with new and exciting insights about the world of work.

New Forms of Expression

Mrs. Landis was tired of seeing the same four or five formats for history projects. Her students, she decided, were "stuck" on posters, dioramas, papers, and time lines as a way of showing what they learned. She invited six adults to visit the class to show students ways they expressed ideas. One man presented a captivating performance as a traveling medicine man. Another demonstrated the art of story telling. A third visitor talked about photojournalism and ways in which students could take or use pictures to reflect insights about history. A fourth visitor combined drama, mime, and music to present ideas. A fifth visitor talked about her use of symposium format to communicate. A final visitor demonstrated effective use of Web sites as a vehicle for sharing ideas. Each presenter left the students with descriptors for a quality presentation in his particular mode of expression.

Mrs. Landis challenged her students to avoid the "favorite four" ways of expressing their learning. Instead, she challenged them to use some of the new formats, or to propose options of their own—with their own proposals for appropriate quality in whatever they proposed. Her goal, she told them, was not so much to have the students try something in which they already knew they were good, but rather to take a chance on forms of expression that would help them see both themselves and history in a new light.

A Few Guidelines for Interest-Based Differentiation

Interests are, in a way, windows on the world. A developed interest in one area is almost inevitably a route to learning about many other things. It's helpful to think about some interest areas that students may have or might be able to develop. It's also a good idea to extend our

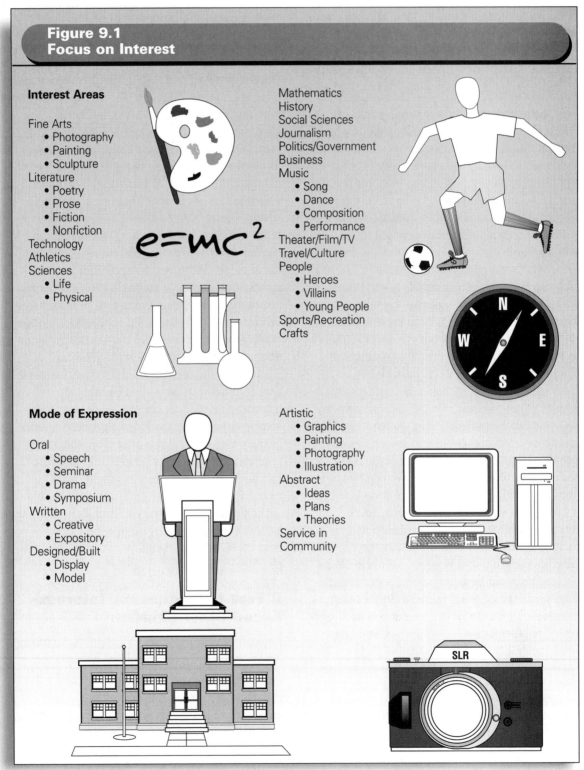

Figure 9.1
Focus on Interest

Interest Areas

Fine Arts
- Photography
- Painting
- Sculpture

Literature
- Poetry
- Prose
- Fiction
- Nonfiction

Technology

Athletics

Sciences
- Life
- Physical

Mathematics
History
Social Sciences
Journalism
Politics/Government
Business

Music
- Song
- Dance
- Composition
- Performance

Theater/Film/TV
Travel/Culture

People
- Heroes
- Villains
- Young People

Sports/Recreation
Crafts

$e=mc^2$

Mode of Expression

Oral
- Speech
- Seminar
- Drama
- Symposium

Written
- Creative
- Expository

Designed/Built
- Display
- Model

Artistic
- Graphics
- Painting
- Photography
- Illustration

Abstract
- Ideas
- Plans
- Theories

Service in
Community

SLR

own awareness of other ways in which people express their ideas, feelings, and skills. Figure 9.1 provides a beginning framework for a teacher to consider options she might present to students for interest-based learning. There's much more that could be added to the figure, however. Feel free to expand it as you go.

There's no single recipe for tapping or expanding student interests, but here are a few pointers to consider. They should make interest-based differentiation more effective.

• **Link interest-based exploration with key components of the curriculum.** There's nothing wrong with an opportunity for students to meander about in an area of interest. In general, however, it's wise for the teacher to provide a bit of focus for the interest-based study. It's likely the curriculum specifies certain concepts, categories, understandings, and skills that students should acquire. If the teacher can help students see how those essential curricular elements are revealed through learning about an interest area, then both the student's goals and the goals of the curriculum can be served simultaneously. Further, common class discussions are much easier if all students explored common understandings and used common skills—even though the interest-based explorations differ.

• **Provide structure likely to lead to student success.** There's often an element of student independence required for interest-based differentiation. That's the case because different students will be pursuing different interests, as opposed to everyone in the class moving lockstep through the curriculum. Some students are highly independent, even at an early age. Others need much more guidance to succeed. In every case, it's the job of the teacher to provide the sort of scaffolding that helps a student grow in independence—even those who are more independent than agemates. Think about elements such as posing questions for inquiry,

setting goals, rubrics, time lines, checkpoints, peer critiques of drafts, miniworkshops on conducting research, or other structures you can develop to ensure that your students work smarter in their interest-based work.

• **Develop efficient ways of sharing interest-based findings.** It's often not the best use of time for each student in a class of 30 to present their work to every other student. That's particularly true if we've not invested time in teaching students how to be compelling presenters. Sharing quads, in which each student presents to three others, may be more effective than whole class sharing. The quads are sometimes most effective when all students in the quad share a common interest. At other times, however, students learn more by sharing with students who explored different interests. You may want to think about having students share interest-based products with adults who have a similar interest. (In that case, have the student find her own audience as part of the product requirements.) Students can create exhibits for perusal by others rather than oral presentation.

• **Create an open invitation for student interests.** One way to contribute to an open and inviting classroom environment is to let students know that you welcome their ideas and want them to let you know what they are interested in. When students know they can propose ideas for tasks and projects and believe you'll help them find a way to expand their own interests, there is a much greater sense of shared ownership of learning. Fortunate students hear teachers say, "Here's an idea I had. How can we make it better?" Or, "Here's something important to learn about. How would you like to come at it?" Or, "What would make this interesting for you?"

• **Keep an open eye and an open mind for the student with a serious passion.** From time to time, there's a student who is on fire to learn about something that's just not part of the curriculum. You may well be the best teacher for that student if you can find a way to let him pursue that passion—even if it means giving up some of what *you* had in mind. For some students, the greatest gift a teacher can give is permission to explore a topic, time to do it, and an interested ear.

Chances are that such a student won't become an academic wreck because she missed one class project or a week of homework or some class discussions. Your affirmation that the student's hunger to learn is worthy of nurturing and trust may count for much more in the long run than a carefully prescribed and rigid curriculum. Besides, you can often embed your agenda in the student's agenda if necessary.

• **Remember that interest-based differentiation can be combined with other types of differentiation.** It's often possible to have a task or product that combines common elements for a whole class, some readiness-based components, some interest-based components, and some learning profile options. Although it's convenient to think about differentiation according to the categories of readiness, interest, and learning profile, it's not necessary to separate the categories in planning or in instruction.

A Glimpse at Strategies That Support Interest Differentiation

There are many instructional strategies that are ready made to support interest-based differentiation. Figure 9.2 lists a number of them. While this book does not afford the opportunity to explore each of the strategies, information is available in educational resources on all of them. Here is a brief overview of a few of the strategies.

I-Search. This process encourages students to be an inquirer on a topic of personal interest based on their experience. The I-Search format helps students learn to uncover their own curiosity, find and use sources (including interviews) helpful in answering their questions, write what they find, and judge the rigor of their own work (Joyce & Tallman, 1997; Macrorie, 1988).

Orbitals. This strategy encourages students to raise questions of interest to them individually, figure out how to find answers to their questions, and devise ways to share their findings with peers. The questions may vary in complexity. The duration of the finding-out process will also vary. Thus students with quite different levels of academic or research sophistication can develop interests with this approach (Stevenson, 1992).

Design-A-Day. Students decide what to work on for a class period or several class periods. They specify goals, set time lines, work toward their goals, and assess their own progress. This strategy is useful when students have a particular interest to pursue or when they'd like to do something they've seen a classmate do during a differentiated class. The strategy is also a good early step in preparing students to succeed with longer and more demanding formats such as learning contracts.

Group Investigation. This cooperative learning strategy is excellent for helping students decide on a topic of personal interest, find out about the topic in defensible ways, work collaboratively, and present findings with confidence. The strategy details the role of the teacher and students in each phase of the investigation (Sharan & Sharan, 1992).

WebQuests. The WebQuest is a teacher-designed Internet lesson developed with specific

Figure 9.2
Strategies That Support Interest-Based Differentiation

- Exploratory studies
- Studying concepts and principles through the lens of interest
- Student choice of tasks
- Independent study
- Orbitals
- Design-A-Day
- I-Searches
- Mentorships/Apprenticeships
- Group Investigation
- Interest groups
- Jigsaw
- Literature circles
- WebQuests
- Negotiated criteria for tasks and products
- Student-selected audiences

Jigsaw. In this cooperative strategy, students work with peers who study one facet of a topic. They then return to a "home-base" group for sharing what they have learned. The home-base group is composed of a student specializing in each facet of the topic. Students in the home-base group are responsible for reporting to the group on their specialty topic and for learning what other students report (Clarke, 1994).

Literature Circles. This student-led discussion format provides excellence guidance that allows students to read on topics of interest and share readings with others who read the same material. It allows teachers to break away comfortably from the sense that all students must read the same materials in order to have meaningful discussions (Daniels, 1994).

Negotiated Criteria. In this format, a teacher may specify some whole-class requirements for product or task success. The student also contributes some criteria of personal interest to her. Finally, the teacher may specify one or more criteria for an individual student.

There's lots of talk in educational circles about creating lifelong learners. It's easy to argue for schools as places where students come to believe that learning is fulfilling, consuming, and deeply satisfying. It's more difficult to realize the goal. Our chances of doing so are greatly enhanced if, as teachers, we cultivate and affirm student interests.

❦ ❦ ❦

The next "how to" chapter goes beyond student interests to encompass learning profiles—styles and intelligences.

learning goals in mind, some specified and relevant Internet links, and guidelines that support students in the research or finding out process. The teacher designs a WebQuest to give individuals or small groups of learners the opportunity to use research, problem solving, and basic skills—as they move through a process of finding out, drawing conclusions about, and developing a product on a topic or question. WebQuests can easily be differentiated by readiness, but are also very well suited to differentiation according to student interest (Kelly, 2000). WebQuest:http://edweb.sdsu.edu/webquest/webquest/html.

THE How To's OF Planning Lessons Differentiated BY Learning Profile

Learning profile refers to ways in which we learn best as individuals. Each of us knows some ways of learning that are quite effective for us, and others that slow us down or make learning feel awkward. Common sense, experience, and research suggest to us that when teachers can tap into routes that promote efficient and effective learning for students, results are better. The goals of learning-profile differentiation are to help individual learners understand modes of learning that work best for them, and to offer those options so that each learner finds a good learning fit in the classroom.

The Categories of Learning-Profile Factors

There are four categories of learning-profile factors, and teachers can use them to plan curriculum and instruction that fit learners. There is

some overlap in the categories, but each has been well researched and found to be important for the learning process. A student's learning style, intelligence preference, gender, and culture can influence learning profile. Figure 10.1 suggests some ways of thinking about learning profiles in students—and ourselves as educators, as well.

Learning-Style Preferences

Learning style refers to environmental or personal factors. Some students may learn best when they can move around, others need to sit still. Some students enjoy a room with lots to look at, color, things to touch and try out. Other students function best when the environment is more "spare" because they find a "busy" classroom distracting. Some students need a great deal of light in a room in order to feel comfortable. Other students prefer a darker room. Some students will learn best through oral modes, others through visual channels, still

Figure 10.1
Focus on Learning Profile

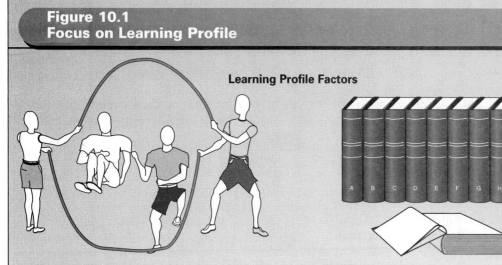

Learning Profile Factors

Group Orientation
independent/self-orientation
group/peer orientation
adult orientation
combination

Learning Environment
quiet/noise
warm/cool
still/mobile
flexible/fixed
"busy"/"spare"

Cognitive Style
creative/conforming
essence/facts
whole-to-part/part-to-whole
expressive/controlled
nonlinear/linear
inductive/deductive
people-oriented/task or object-oriented
concrete/abstract
collaboration/competition
interpersonal/introspective
easily distracted/long attention span
group achievement/personal achievement
oral/visual/kinesthetic
reflective/action-oriented

Intelligence Preference
analytic
practical
creative
verbal/linguistic
logical/mathematical
spatial/visual
bodily/kinesthetic
musical/rhythmic
interpersonal
intrapersonal
naturalist
existential

others through touch or movement. Although a teacher cannot manipulate all these elements, and other learning style components, all the time, it is possible for a teacher to give students some learning choices. It's also possible for a teacher to create a room with different "looks" in different portions of the room, or with differing working arrangements.

Intelligence Preferences

Intelligence preference refers to the sorts of brain-based predispositions we all have for learning. Two theorist/researchers have proposed ways of thinking about intelligence preferences. Howard Gardner (1993) suggests that we each have varying strengths in combinations of intelligences he calls verbal linguistic, logical mathematical, visual spatial, musical rhythmic, bodily kinesthetic, interpersonal, intrapersonal, and naturalistic—and perhaps existential. Robert Sternberg (1985) suggests that we all have varying strengths in combinations of intelligences he refers to as analytic (schoolhouse intelligence, preference for learning in linear ways often typical of school), practical (contextual intelligence, preference for seeing how and why things work in the world as people actually use them), and creative (problem-solving intelligence, preference for making new connections, innovation). Indications are that when students approach learning in ways that address their intelligence preferences, results are quite positive.

Culture-Influenced Preferences

Culture affects how we learn, as well. It can influence whether we see time as fixed and rigid or flexible and fluid, whether we are more effusive or reserved in expressing emotions, whether we learn best in a whole-to-part or a part-to-whole approach, whether we prefer to learn material that's contextual and personal or discrete and impersonal, whether we prefer to

work with a group or individually, whether we most value creativity or conformity, whether we are more reflective or more impulsive—and many other preferences that can greatly affect learning. Also some learning patterns may differ from one culture to another; there is huge learning variance within every culture.

The goal of the teacher is, therefore, not to suggest that individuals from a particular culture ought to learn in a particular way, but rather to come to understand the great range of learning preferences that will exist in any group of people and to create a classroom flexible enough to invite individuals to work in ways they find most productive.

Gender-Based Preferences

Gender also influences how we learn. As is the case with culture, there are learning patterns in each gender—but great variance, as well. Whereas more males than females may prefer competitive learning, for example, some males will prefer collaborative learning and some females will prefer competition. Some of the same elements that are influenced by culture can also be influenced by gender (for example, expressiveness versus reserve, group versus individual orientation, analytic versus creative or practical thinking, and so on).

Combined Preferences

Combinations of culture and gender will create unique constellations of learning preferences in individuals. Patterns of learning preference are certainly complex when we look at an individual's learning style; intelligence; culture-influenced, gender-influenced preferences. A sensitive teacher understands that her students may have learning preferences much like or much different than that of the teacher and tries to create options and choices that make everyone comfortable much of the time.

Some Guidelines for Learning-Profile Differentiation

Though there is no single way of ensuring that students get to learn in ways that work best for them, some guidelines are broadly useful in establishing classrooms responsive to a wide range of learning preferences.

• **Remember that some, but not all, of your students share your learning preferences.** For example, if you are a highly auditory learner, you may be prone to be an auditory teacher, as well. That's great for kids who learn like you do, but not great for kids with visual or kinesthetic learning preferences. If you were successful in school, you may find analytic and part-to-whole learning a breeze. Some students in your class will like those approaches as well, but students who need more creative, contextual, and whole-to-part approaches may feel like they are working in a fog unless you stretch your own comfort zone and teaching repertoire.

• **Help your students reflect on their own preferences.** Give your students a vocabulary of learning-profile options. Let them know you're offering creative, practical, and analytic learning choices today—or that you've intentionally created both competitive and collaborative study formats—or that you're making a connection between whole-to-part (global, big idea) and part-to-whole (detail) portions of today's lab. Then invite students to talk about which approaches make learning most natural and effective for them. That's also a good opportunity to help students realize that not everyone in the class learns the same way, and that a good teacher works hard to honor many routes to learning, rather than only one.

• **Use both teacher-structured and student-choice avenues to learning-profile differentiation.** Sometimes it's really effective for a teacher to think about using several intelligences as ways for students to explore or express ideas. Often, only the teacher can ensure flexible use of time or combination of presentation modes. Even when a teacher does not have time to structure or craft several learning-profile options for a lesson, much can be accomplished by asking students to make their own choices. Students can select modes of expression and decide whether to work alone or with a peer, to sit in a desk or curl up on the floor with a book, to accept inevitable classroom sounds or screen them out by using earplugs or headphones, and so on. When students are partners with teachers in making the learning environment a good fit, more is accomplished with less strain on the teacher.

• **Select a few learning-profile categories for emphasis as you begin.** We know a great deal about learning preferences—so much, in fact, that it can seem overwhelming. As you begin to differentiate your instruction in response to a range of learning-profile needs, select a few categories to emphasize in your planning. You may, for example, work with Sternberg's (1985) three intelligences as you create tasks; using both contextual and factual illustrations for your students, you may employ both visual and auditory approaches to sharing information with your students. That's enough to begin. Then, whenever possible, offer your students learning decisions that they can make to further craft the classroom to match their learning needs.

• **Be a student of your students.** It's very hard to "get inside someone else's skin." It's devilishly difficult to see life as someone who experiences the world differently than you do. We particularly fail many students whose cultural background is different from our own. It's essential to watch individuals in your class for learning clues, to talk with them about what works and doesn't work for them, and to invite them to make suggestions or pose alternatives that seem more promising. It's also useful to ask parents to provide insights into what works, or doesn't, when their students learn. If we can expand our vision beyond the parameters of our own private universe, we become more welcoming and effective teachers of children who inevitably inhabit private universes different from our own.

A Glimpse at Strategies That Support Learning-Profile Differentiation

There are numerous instructional strategies that help us focus on students' learning-profile needs. Figure 10.2 lists a number of them. Here are brief explanations of a few strategies helpful in differentiating instruction in response to students' learning profiles.

Complex Instruction. This powerful strategy emphasizes teachers studying their students to determine which intellectual strengths each student brings to the classroom. The teacher then designs high-level, complex learning tasks that draw on the intellectual strengths of each student in a collaborative group (Cohen, 1994).

Entry Points. It is possible to encourage students to enter a topic or explore it through a learning preference (Gardner, 1993), thus making early experiences a good fit. Entry point explorations can be narrational (telling a story), quantitative (scientific approaches), foundational (looking at beliefs or frameworks of meaning at the core of the topic), aesthetic (sensory, arts-based approaches), or experiential (hands-on, personal opportunities to become involved).

4-MAT. This approach to planning suggests that varied learners would prefer (1) mastery of

information, (2) understanding of key ideas, (3) personal involvement, or (4) creating something new related to a topic. A teacher using 4-MAT plans lesson sequences on a given topic in which each of the four preferences is stressed. This ensures that every student experiences the topic through a preferred approach and also has opportunities to strengthen learning in less preferred modes (McCarthy, 1996).

Varied Approaches to Organizing Ideas. It's important that students organize their thinking so they can make sense of ideas, communicate clearly, and retain and retrieve information. Often it's less important which approach to organization a student uses than that they have an organizational approach that works for them. When there's no compelling reason why all students must use the same organizational approach, encourage students to select from strategies such as summarizing, mind-mapping, concept mapping, storyboarding, or outlining. Of course, you'll have to ensure that all students understand the various options; but once that's accomplished, you'll quickly see some students gravitate to one approach while other students make different decisions. It's likely to be a learning-profile issue.

Using Learning Profile to Differentiate Content, Process, and Product

As is true for readiness and interest, attending to learning profile provides teachers with a way to differentiate content, process, and product. Here are some examples.

❦ ❦ ❦

Ms. Lide sometimes differentiates content in ways likely to tap in to student-learning profile. She tape-records key materials (or has others do the recording) so that auditory learners can lis-

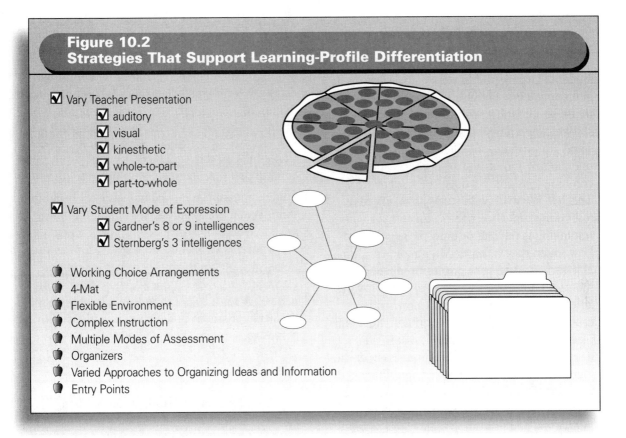

Figure 10.2
Strategies That Support Learning-Profile Differentiation

☑ Vary Teacher Presentation
    ☑ auditory
    ☑ visual
    ☑ kinesthetic
    ☑ whole-to-part
    ☑ part-to-whole

☑ Vary Student Mode of Expression
    ☑ Gardner's 8 or 9 intelligences
    ☑ Sternberg's 3 intelligences

🍎 Working Choice Arrangements
🍎 4-Mat
🍎 Flexible Environment
🍎 Complex Instruction
🍎 Multiple Modes of Assessment
🍎 Organizers
🍎 Varied Approaches to Organizing Ideas and Information
🍎 Entry Points

ten rather than being solely dependent on visual contact with materials. She also sometimes uses role-play just after the students have completed reading, asking students to volunteer to act out what they have read. She finds that kinesthetic learners like this more physical approach to comprehension. When introducing ideas to her students, she makes sure to use graphic organizers to show them how parts of their study fit the big picture of meaning. She also makes certain that she uses an overhead projector or flip chart as she talks so that students can hear and see ideas.

🌱 🌱 🌱

In differentiating process or activities, Mr. Larsen uses what he calls Menus for Success. He might, for example, offer students four ways to explore a math concept today. One approach might ask students to use words and pictures to create directions for how to solve the kind of problem that's the focus of the unit. A second approach might provide multiple versions of the problem to practice, with the opportunity to check answers for accuracy as they go along. A third option might entail students investigating how the kind of math problem could be used to solve a real-life dilemma. A fourth approach might ask students to use manipulatives and words to demonstrate how the problem type works. Whatever the student's selection, they then decide whether they work more effectively alone or with a peer. Mr. Larsen talks with students about learning to make wise selections from the Menu for Success to support healthy learning, just as they would from a restaurant menu to support healthy living.

❦ ❦ ❦

In differentiating products in response to student learning profile, Ms. Michaels uses several approaches. Because she believes her goal is to assess student growth in ways that let each student show how much they know, understand, and can do, she often uses more than one kind of end-of-unit assessment. She may combine tests and portfolios of student work. This lets her work with students on effective test taking, but also enables students for whom test taking is difficult or uninspiring to show how much they've learned in a more comfortable format. When she creates product assignments for students, she nearly always provides at least two or three choices of how students can express what they have learned—for example, through a museum exhibit that includes models and narratives, through an essay or dialogue, or through an annotated and illustrated time line. She also tries to vary research materials to include artifacts, visuals, print materials, interviews, and technology. She varies working arrangements so students sometimes work alone, sometimes with peers, and sometimes in whichever format they prefer.

There are many ways to accommodate students' preferred ways of learning. Looking for a good learning fit for students means, at least in part, trying to understand *how* individuals learn and responding appropriately.

Bringing the Elements Together

In the early stages of differentiation, it's helpful to think about using student readiness, interest, and learning profile to differentiate content, process, and product. Breaking down the task into elements not only lets us focus on smaller and more manageable pieces of teaching, but can also help us assess the degree to which we are looking broadly or narrowly at addressing students' learning needs.

In the end, however, the goal is to have a flow of differentiation so that much of what we do is a fit for each student much of the time (see figures 10.3 and 10.4). That means our goal is to bring together the elements we can differentiate and ways we can go about differentiating them so that there is wholeness to what we do.

A teacher whose skills of differentiation are fluid continually asks, "Would students benefit from flexibility in approaching today's learning goals?" When the answer is yes, the teacher seeks alternative avenues to learning for her students, and invites them to join her in that quest. (see figure 10.5 for sample diagnostic questionnaires). Here's a brief example of an elementary teacher's classroom in which differentiation is pervasive.

❦ ❦ ❦

Mrs. Chen and her students are studying explorers and exploration. As she selects reading material for them, she makes sure to find selections with a wide range of readability. Sometimes she and the class will read a piece in common. Sometimes she will assign materials to particular students. Sometimes they will select what to read. In this way, she hopes to take into account common needs of the whole class as well as both reading readiness and interests of individuals.

As she plans activities, Mrs. Chen envisions both similar readiness groups for some tasks and mixed readiness groups for others. For example, when students are honing their writing skills, they may work with students who have similar goals at a given time. On the other hand, when they write scenarios to depict the challenges faced by explorers, she will form groups that include students who have good ideas, students with a flair for the dramatic, students who write well, and students who are leaders.

Figure 10.3
Before and After: The Flow of Instruction (A Secondary Example)

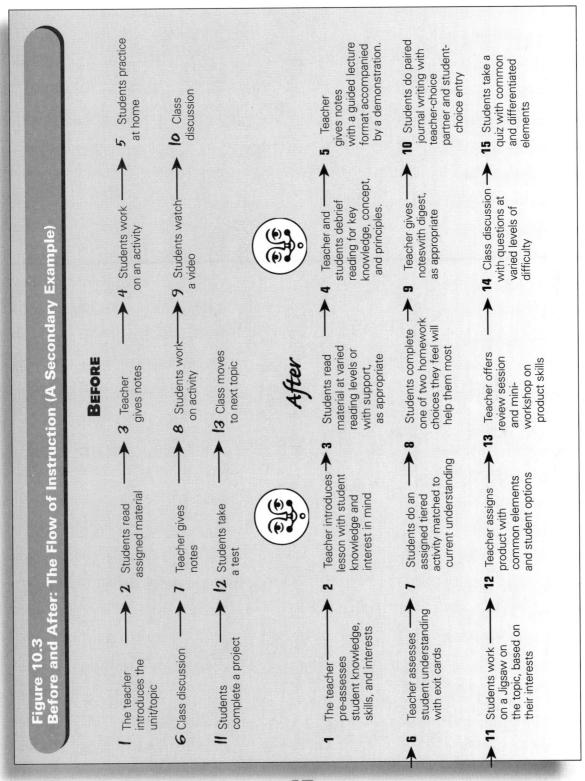

Figure 10.4
Before and After: The Flow of Instruction (A Math Example)

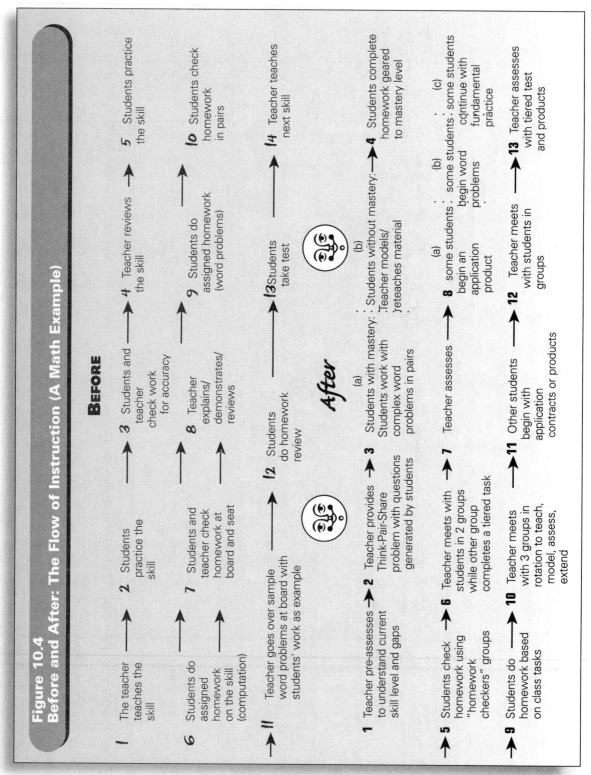

BEFORE

1 The teacher teaches the skill →
2 Students practice the skill →
3 Students and teacher check work for accuracy →
4 Teacher reviews the skill →
5 Students practice the skill

6 Students do assigned homework on the skill (computation) →
7 Students and teacher check homework at board and seat →
8 Teacher explains/demonstrates/reviews →
9 Students do assigned homework (word problems) →
10 Students check homework in pairs

11 Teacher goes over sample word problems at board with students' work as example →
12 Students do homework review →
13 Students take test →
14 Teacher teaches next skill

After

1 Teacher pre-assesses to understand current skill level and gaps →
2 Teacher provides Think-Pair-Share problem with questions generated by students →
3 Students with mastery: Students work with complex word problems in pairs (a)

Students without mastery: Teacher models/reteaches material (b) →
4 Students complete homework geared to mastery level

5 Students check homework using "homework checkers" groups →
6 Teacher meets with students in 2 groups while other group completes a tiered task →
7 Teacher assesses (a)

8 some students: begin an application product (a)

some students: begin word problems (b)

some students: continue with fundamental practice (c)

9 Students do homework based on class tasks →
10 Teacher meets with 3 groups in rotation to teach, model, assess, extend →
11 Other students begin with application contracts or products →
12 Teacher meets with students in groups →
13 Teacher assesses with tiered test and products

Figure 10.5
Diagnosing Student Readiness, Interest, and Learning Profile

Interest Questionnaire: What Do You Want to Learn About Rome?

These are some of the topics we will be studying in our unit on Ancient Rome. We want to know what you want to learn about. Number your choices from 1 to 8. Make sure that 1 is your favorite and 8 is your least favorite.

____ geography

____ government (laws)

____ agriculture (foods they grew)

____ architecture (buildings)

____ music and art

____ religion and sports

____ roles of men, women, and children

____ other (please tell us more)

Readiness Questionnaire: What Can You Tell Us About Rome?

1. What country is Rome in?

2. What does "civilization" mean?

3. Give some examples of different civilizations.

4. Name any famous Roman people.

5. Many things in our country and culture came from the Romans. What can you think of?

Source: Developed by Denise Murphy and Beth Ann Potter.

—continued

Figure 10.5 (CONTINUED)
Diagnosing Student Readiness, Interest and Learning Profile

Learning Profile Qeustionnaire: How Do You Like to Learn?

1. I study best when it is quiet. ☐ yes ☐ no

2. I am able to ignore the noise of other people talking while I am working. ☐ yes ☐ no

3. I like to work at a table or desk. ☐ yes ☐ no

4. I like to work on the floor. ☐ yes ☐ no

5. I work hard for myself. ☐ yes ☐ no

6. I work hard for my parents or teacher. ☐ yes ☐ no

7. I will work on an assignment until it is completed no matter what. ☐ yes ☐ no

8. Sometimes I get frustrated with my work and do not finish it. ☐ yes ☐ no

9. When my teacher gives an assignment, I like to have exact steps on how to complete it. ☐ yes ☐ no

10. When my teacher gives an assignment, I like to create my own steps on how to complete it. ☐ yes ☐ no

11. I like to work by myself. ☐ yes ☐ no

12. I like to work in pairs or in groups. ☐ yes ☐ no

13. I like to have an unlimited amount of itime to work on an assignment. ☐ yes ☐ no

14. I like to have a certain amount of time to work on an assignment. ☐ yes ☐ no

15. I like to learn by moving and doing. ☐ yes ☐ no

16. I like to learn while sitting at my desk. ☐ yes ☐ no

Source: Developed by Denise Murphy and Beth Ann Potter.

As the unit ends, students will demonstrate their learning in part through "exchanges" between past explorers and contemporary explorers. All students are responsible for demonstrating designated knowledge, understandings, and skills. The teacher will assign each student a past explorer based on the quantity and availability of research material that is available in the school on the various explorers. Students will select their own contemporary explorer from a teacher-provided list to which students can add names. Here students will make selections based on personal interests, such as science, sports, writing, technology, television, and so on. Students may work alone on their tasks, with one partner, or with a group of three to four students. Individuals and groups then select the format for their explorer exchange. Among choices are a live symposium or dialogue format, a pair of Web pages, a videotaped conversation, a set of letters exchanged between the two, and so on.

There's certainly whole-class instruction in Mrs. Chen's room, but chances are that whole-class instruction will be followed by opportunities for students to come to grips with ideas and skills on their own terms. Chances are also good that there is flexibility built in to much of what goes on so that each student feels the classroom "belongs" to him.

Figures 10.3 and 10.4 provide two more examples of the flow in a differentiated classroom where all the elements come together. In both instances events in the classroom are first presented as they might occur in a one-size-fits-all version, then are re-presented as they might look in a classroom where the teacher honors and plans for individual learning needs.

Diagnosing Student Interest, Readiness, and Learning Profile

Although there are many published tools to help teachers determine student readiness, interest, and learning profile, sometimes it's most economical to begin with common sense and a little teacher ingenuity. Figure 10.5 provides one such example.

Two beginning teachers understood their need to match what they were about to teach to students whom they did not yet know well. As they began an elementary unit on Ancient Rome, the teachers developed a three-part assessment based on students' prior knowledge about what they were going to teach (readiness) and questions the teachers felt comfortable addressing related to interest and learning profile. You'll see that the format of the assessment is simple and straightforward. It's also clear that the knowledge about students that the teachers gleaned from this multipart assessment gave them lots to work with as they began to plan their unit to ensure its match for their learners.

Remember that everything students do is a potential source of information about their current understanding and skills, what they like to learn about, and how they learn best. Consider the possibility that you can learn a great deal about students by using simple teacher-made tools and by observing and reflecting on data that are around you every day.

❦ ❦ ❦

In the next chapter, we shift our focus from students to the content of the curriculum (but keep in mind all we have learned from our students).

Differentiating Content

It is difficult and somewhat unnatural to carve apart the curricular elements of content, process, and product, because students process ideas as they read content, think while they create products, and conjure ideas for products while they encounter ideas in the materials they use. Nonetheless, thinking about how to differentiate instruction is more manageable by examining one element at a time. Just proceed with the awareness that these elements are more interconnected than they may sound here.

Content is the "input" of teaching and learning. It's what we teach or what we want students to learn.

Differentiating content can be thought of in two ways. First, in differentiating content, we can adapt *what* we teach. Second, we can adapt or modify *how we give students access* to what we want them to learn. For example, if I ask some students to begin work with fractions in 3rd grade, while others are working hard to master division, I have differentiated *what* the students are learning. Similarly, I may elect to assign students to spelling based on their current spelling skills rather than having all students work with a 4th grade spelling program when some of the learners spell at a 1st grade level and some at a high school level. On the other hand, I keep what students learn relatively the same and change how I give them *access* to it if I encourage advanced students to read a novel rapidly and with independence while I find additional time for struggling readers to read the same novel, and use peer partners to support their reading as well.

In general, there is benefit to holding *what* students learn relatively steady, while changing how we give access to the content to match student needs. Sometimes, however, it seems to make better sense to change *what* we teach as well. The latter is especially sensible when we are teaching a linear progression of skills, such as spelling or math computation.

Differentiating Content for Student Need

Content can be differentiated in response to a student's readiness level, interests, or learning profile. It can also be differentiated in response to any combination of readiness, interest, and learning profile.

• **Readiness differentiation** of content has as its goal matching the material or information students are asked to learn to a student's capacity to read and understand it. For example, it is a poor use of time to ask a 5th grade student who reads independently at a 9th grade-level to do most of her work in a grade-level reading series. It is equally inappropriate to ask a student who speaks and reads little English to read independently from a grade-level U.S. History book. One way of thinking about readiness differentiation of content is to use "The Equalizer" (Figure 8.1, page 47) as a guide, asking yourself if materials are at an appropriately challenging level of complexity, independence, pacing, and so on.

• **Interest differentiation** of content involves including in the curriculum ideas and materials that build on current student interests or extend student interests. For example, an English teacher encourages a budding young comedienne to read selections that involve humor. A history teacher helps a student find Web sites that feed his curiosity about the role of Native Americans in the Civil War.

• **Learning profile differentiation** of content implies ensuring that a student has a way of "coming at" materials and ideas that match his preferred way of learning. For instance, some students may handle a lecture best if the teacher uses overhead transparencies as well as talk—linking visual and auditory learning. Some students will comprehend reading far better if they can read aloud—whereas other students need silence when they read. Reading the science text may be just the ticket to help one student understand the concept of "work," while another student may grasp the idea better by watching a demonstration that uses exemplars of "work" and "not work."

By way of example, students in a middle school science class are beginning work on the characteristics of mammals. Today, the teacher has planned several approaches for introducing her students to key concepts, terms, and ideas about mammals. First, students selected which of five vertebrates they'd rather investigate (differentiation of content based on student interest). Then the teacher gave each investigation team several ways to learn about the mammal selected by group members. For each mammal, there is a small box of books at varied reading levels (differentiation by readiness). In addition, there are either audio or video tapes about each mammal, and bookmarked Web sites as well (differentiation according to student-learning profile).

Further, students can take "freelance" notes on their reading, or use a teacher-provided matrix to guide note taking (differentiation in response to student readiness). This is an example of a teacher who is differentiating content in several ways. Here, she is holding steady the key concepts, ideas, and skills (*what* she wants her students to learn), and modifying how she ensures effective *access* to the "input" she has defined as essential.

Strategies for Differentiating Content

Here are some strategies for differentiating content. Some of them are useful in differentiating what we need students to learn. Many are useful in differentiating how we ensure appropriate access to what we need students to learn. Most can be used to differentiate content by readiness, interest, and learning profile.

Concept-Based Teaching

In many classrooms, students "cover" lots of facts, vocabulary words, names, dates, and rules. Unfortunately, they also forget much of what they "learn" as they leave that information behind and move on to another topic or lesson. Much of this "memory loss" occurs because they never really understood or saw the purpose of what they learned. Rather than slogging through a swamp of facts, you can help your students better understand and see utility in an area of study by emphasizing its key concepts and principles. Concepts are the building blocks of meaning.

Instead of spending a month memorizing categories of animals or studying penguins, students can use that same time to study patterns in the animal kingdom, talk about traits, use traits to identify and classify animals, and learn how to predict traits from habitats or vice versa. "Patterns" is a concept that undergirds how scientists look at and classify things. Having students become adept at determining and predicting patterns and using those patterns to think about various forms of life helps them (1) understand rather than memorize, (2) retain ideas and facts longer because they are more meaningful, (3) make connections between subjects and facets of a single subject, (4) relate ideas to their own lives, and (5) build networks of meaning for effectively dealing with future knowledge.

Differentiated instruction is so powerful because it focuses on concepts and principles instead of predominantly on facts. Teachers who differentiate instruction offer minimal drill and practice of facts (as these practices tend to create little meaning or power for future learning); they focus instead on essential and meaningful understandings to create transferable learning power.

One elementary teacher uses a differentiated unit to study the concept of extinction. Her class explores two key principles: (1) extinction can come about because of natural changes in the environment, and (2) extinction can come about because of human-made changes in the environment. One group uses dinosaurs as an example of extinction and investigates changes that may have caused their extinction. Another group compares the dinosaurs' extinction to today's rain forests, looking for similarities and differences in extinction patterns. Both groups encounter powerful scientific principles, specific examples, and a need to hypothesize and draw conclusions. But one group studies this content in a more foundational, concrete, single-faceted way, while the other group conducts an exploration that is more transformational, abstract, and multifaceted. The teacher proactively matches the "equalizer buttons" of the tasks and materials to each group's current learning needs.

Being sure of key concepts and principles in what you teach is a great way to begin thinking about differentiation. It also makes your teaching more relevant and potent in general.

Curriculum Compacting

This strategy was developed by Joe Renzulli at the University of Connecticut and is specifically designed to help advanced learners maximize their use of time for learning (Rezis & Renzulli, 1992). Compacting is a three-stage process.

In **Stage 1**, the teacher identifies students who are candidates for compacting and assesses what they know and do not know about a particular topic or chapter. Students may request compacting or the teacher may decide to "compact" a student.

Initial assessment occurs either prior to or early in the study. Assessment may be formal, such as a written post-test; or informal, such as the teacher and student having a focused conversation about the subject being studied. Following this assessment, the teacher notes which skills and understandings each student has reasonably mastered (i.e., knowing 70–75 percent or more of the content). Students who are compacting are exempt from whole-class instruction and activities in content areas they have already mastered, thus "buying time" for learning more challenging and interesting material.

In **Stage 2,** the teacher notes any skills or understandings covered in the study in which the student did not demonstrate mastery, and then lays out a plan to make certain the student learns those things. The plan may require the student to join other classmates for particular portions of the study, do homework that provides practice on missing skills, or demonstrate mastery of those skills in a product that is created in the third and final stage of the compacting process.

At the beginning of **Stage 3**, the teacher and student design an investigation or study for the student to engage in while others are working with the general lessons. The teacher and student together agree on the project's parameters, goals, time lines, procedures for completing the tasks, criteria for evaluation, and any other necessary elements. The student does not have to reinvest freed-up time in the same subject from which he was compacted. One student who compacts out of math, for example, may elect to spend his time working on a project in a special interest area such as science fiction. Or, if he especially likes math, he might want to develop a plan for using advanced mathematics software available in class.

Keeping records when using compacting has three benefits: (1) teachers demonstrate accountability for student learning, (2) parents understand why it is advantageous for their children to work with an alternate task, and (3) students develop awareness of their specific learning profiles.

Advanced learners gain little by continuing to relearn the known, but they gain much from the expectation that they will continually engage in challenging and productive learning in school. Compacting helps eliminate the former and facilitate the latter.

Using Varied Text and Resource Materials

Grade-level texts are often far too simple for some students in a given class, and yet too complex for others. Using multiple texts and combining them with a wide variety of other supplementary materials increases your chances for reaching all your students with content that is meaningful to them as individuals. You can develop valuable differentiation resources by building a classroom library from discarded texts of various levels (or requesting that textbook money be used to buy three classroom sets of different books rather than one copy of a single text for everyone), and by collecting magazines, newsletters, brochures, and other print materials.

The rich array of materials available through the Internet makes it far easier than once was the case for a teacher to differentiate materials based on student need. Other things being equal, advanced learners will usually use advanced resources, but may occasionally find it helpful, when beginning a complex study, to find out about a topic in the more straightforward presentation found in a less-challenging source. Likewise, struggling learners may from time to time grasp an idea better by looking at diagrams or pictures in a more advanced source.

As students' task needs vary, so should their use of resources. Many computer programs present increasing levels of challenge and complexity. In math or science, some students may need to use manipulatives to understand a concept, while others can move directly from an explanation or reading to abstract use of that concept without working with manipulatives. Some videos present key ideas with clarity, others extend explorations with greater breadth and depth than may be desirable for students less advanced with that topic. For students learning English while they learn other curriculum, it would be of major assistance to read ideas first in their native language, then in English. The key is to match the levels of complexity, abstractness, depth, breadth, and so forth of the resource materials with the student's learning needs. Don't forget that text and other materials can also be used in response to a student's interests as well as in response to current learner readiness or learning profile.

Learning Contracts

Learning contracts between teachers and students come in several varieties. One allows students some freedom in their use of class time in exchange for doing responsible and effective work. Contracts can contain both "skills" and "content" components, and are helpful in managing differentiated classrooms because the components of a contract can vary with a student's needs.

For example, students in a 4th grade class are all using contracts. Jake's specifies that during contract time in the week ahead he must complete his next two spelling lists, master two levels on the computer program on division by one digit, and work with the characterization project from a novel of his choosing. Jake's spelling lists are a bit above grade level, reflecting his comfort as a speller. Because his math work is below grade level, extra time with the computer may help him move along more confidently. The novel Jake selects can be based on his interests, and his task with it—thinking and writing about himself in comparison to the main character—has been designed to help him think through the key strategies a writer uses to build characters.

Jenny has also made a contract that includes spelling, computer work, and a novel. Rather than a spelling list, she uses an advanced vocab-

ulary strategy because she spells several years above grade level. Jenny will use the computer program to practice division by three digits. She will also select a novel that she likes, analyze the main character, and create an opposite or mirror image character by applying traits of characterization.

Both students get to map out their plan of action for the week, decide which tasks will be done in school and which at home, and progress at a rate and depth of content challenging for them. Both are accountable for their time and self-management, and understand that their teacher will assign them work if they violate their contract obligations. Jake and Jenny share a table with two friends whose contracts differ somewhat from theirs.

Contracts combine a sense of shared goals with individual appropriateness and an independent work format. They also give the teacher time for conferences and small-group or individual work sessions based on progress and needs.

Minilessons

When a teacher introduces a concept to the whole class, chances are that some students will grasp it instantly (or could have skipped the lesson because they already have mastered the idea, skill, or information). On the other hand, some students will be foggy or lost in relation to the "input" the teacher had given them. In such cases, minilessons can be a valuable way to differentiate content.

Based on assessment of student understanding, the teacher may reteach a part of her students, find another way of teaching a group of students, or meet with yet another group to extend their understanding and skill. Minilessons can be quite effective in targeting content to students' readiness, interests, or learning profile.

Varied Support Systems

You can make content of varying complexity levels more accessible to your students by using a variety of support systems, such as study buddies, reading partners, audio and video recorders, and peer and adult mentors. These strategies can help many students stretch their capacities as learners.

Reading Partners and **Audio/Video Recorders.** A 5th grader can be great at audio-taping books for 2nd graders who need assistance with their reading. A 3rd grader who records a grade-level book can help create enriching materials for a classmate who has trouble decoding or reading long passages. High school students can create tapes summarizing journal articles on a particular topic to give advanced 6th graders access to materials beyond the scope of their classroom or school library. Some of those 6th graders can help 4th graders learn how to make a speech by making a video on the subject. An advanced 4th grader can make a video on the types of buildings in the community, which could then be used in a kindergarten learning center.

Note-Taking Organizers. Some students, even of older ages, find it very difficult to read text or listen to a lecture and come away with a coherent sense of what it was all about. For such students, it can be quite useful to work with a visual organizer that follows the flow of ideas from the text or lecture. Not only might such organizers help them focus on key ideas and information, but they may also help some learners see how a teacher or author develops a line of thought. Remember, however, that students who read independently may find it restrictive to have to use such organizers. The point is always to provide individual learners with a support system that helps the student grow—not one that feels like an impediment.

Highlighted Print Materials. A teacher can highlight critical passages in text or supplementary materials, keeping several copies of the highlighted materials in the teacher's desk. When a student has difficulty managing an entire chapter or article, the teacher can easily provide that student with a highlighted version. From the outside, the material looks like everyone else's, but because of the highlighting, the student can expend energy on reading and understanding essential portions of the chapter rather than becoming discouraged with what seems like an insurmountable amount of print.

Digests of Key Ideas. Most effective teachers could, with minimal expenditure of time, create a one- or two-page capsule of ideas in a unit. Such a digest can be of great assistance to students who struggle with print materials, lectures, or even organization of information. The digest could be in the form of sentences and paragraphs, a flow chart or concept map of the unit or topic, or a combination. It might also spotlight key vocabulary and provide essential questions the unit is designed to address. Such digests also help teachers clarify their own thinking about the core of a unit or topic.

Peer and Adult Mentors. Adults often volunteer to help youngsters who are behind with their work and in need of additional guidance. All learners—not just those who are struggling—benefit from time with adults who can answer questions about shared interests, sharpen their thinking, or give them access to advanced research skills. A bright 5th grader can also be a great mentor for an advanced 3rd grader who shares similar interests. You can create extensive support systems by using the people and technologies in your classroom, school, and community, thus giving everyone a chance to reach higher, learn more, and contribute to one another's learning.

❦ ❦ ❦

No doubt you have other ways to match content to learner readiness, interest, and learning profile that work well for you and your students. The goal when differentiating content is to offer approaches to "input" (information, ideas, and skills) that meet students individually where they are and vigorously support their forward progress. The next chapter provides ideas for using varied processes in instruction.

Differentiating Process

Process means sense-making or, just as it sounds, opportunity for learners to process the content or ideas and skills to which they have been introduced. When students encounter new ideas, information, or skills, they need time to run the input through their own filters of meaning. As they try to analyze, apply, question, or solve a problem using the material, they have to make sense of it before it becomes "theirs." This processing or sense-making is an essential component of instruction because, without it, students either lose the ideas or confuse them.

In the language of school, process is often spoken of as an activity. It's probably wisest to use the term "sense-making activity" to remind ourselves that an activity achieves maximum power as a vehicle for learning only when it is squarely focused on a portion of something essential that students need to know, understand, and be able to do as a result of a particular study.

Students who already understand how to convert fractions into decimals don't need to do an activity designed to help them make sense of the underlying principles; they have already processed and made sense of those ideas. Students who are foggy about fractions aren't ready to benefit from a sense-making activity on converting fractions into decimals; they need an activity that helps them further clarify the conceptual notion of whole and part that is the underpinning of fractions.

Any effective activity is essentially a sense-making process, designed to help a student progress from a current point of understanding to a more complex level of understanding. Students process and make sense of ideas and information most easily when their classroom activities

• are interesting to the students,
• call on the students to think at a high level, and
• cause the students to use a key skill(s) to understand a key idea(s).

Good differentiated activities are first good *activities*—those that have the characteristics noted above. What makes them differentiated is that the teacher offers more than one way to make sense of what's important. In fact, one way of thinking about the relationship between a good activity and a good differentiated activity is this:

A GOOD ACTIVITY is something students will make or do

- using an essential skill(s) and essential information
- in order to understand an essential idea/principle or answer an essential question.

A GOOD *DIFFERENTIATED* ACTIVITY is something students will make or do

- in a range of modes at varied degrees of sophistication in varying time spans
- with varied amounts of teacher or peer support (scaffolding)
- using an essential skill(s) and essential information
- to understand an essential idea/principle or answer an essential question.

As is the case with content, process or sense-making can be differentiated in response to student readiness, interest, and learning profile:

- Differentiating process according to student *readiness* means matching the complexity of a task to a student's current level of understanding and skill.
- Differentiating process according to student *interest* involves giving students choices about facets of a topic in which to specialize or helping them link a personal interest to a sense-making goal.
- Differentiating process according to student learning profile generally means encourag-

ing students to make sense of an idea in a preferred way of learning—for example, exploring or expressing what they learn kinesthetically, or spatially, or verbally, or creatively; or deciding to work alone versus with a partner; or sitting on the floor to do work versus sitting in a straight chair.

Other chapters in the book more fully explore differentiation according to readiness, interest, and learning profile.

Strategies That Support Differentiated Processing

Many instructional strategies (see Figure 12.1) invite teachers to have students work in small groups or independently. Using those strategies makes it easier for a teacher to reach out to individuals and to match activities or process to needs of individuals. Whole-class instruction does not issue such an invitation. Though it's both fun and useful for a teacher to become comfortable with a wide range of instructional strategies that invite flexible teaching, it's crucial to remember that it's the quality and focus of *what* students do that is most important.

The following are among the scores of strategies educators have developed that invite more flexible and responsive sense-making: learning logs, journals, graphic organizers, creative problem solving, cubing, learning centers, interest centers or interest groups, learning contracts, Literature Circles, role playing, cooperative controversy (in which students argue both sides of an issue), choice boards, Jigsaw, think-pair-share, mind-mapping, PMI (listing pluses, minuses, and interesting points about a topic under consideration), model making, and labs.

Tiered assignments or parallel tasks at varied levels of difficulty are also powerful vehicles for differentiating process. Each strategy engages your students in a different thinking or processing response. Sense-making activities are most effective for students when that response

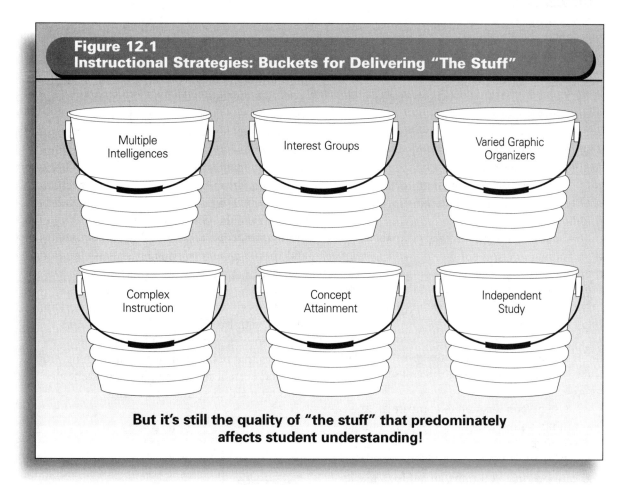

Figure 12.1
Instructional Strategies: Buckets for Delivering "The Stuff"

Multiple Intelligences

Interest Groups

Varied Graphic Organizers

Complex Instruction

Concept Attainment

Independent Study

But it's still the quality of "the stuff" that predominately affects student understanding!

matches their learning needs, as well as specified learning goals.

These instructional strategies are ideal for offering differentiated sense-making or processing options for students in mixed-ability classrooms. The following two scenarios show how teachers use some of these strategies to help their students process and "own" key ideas in ways that work best for them.

❦ ❦ ❦

Mr. Jackson and Cubing

Students in Mr. Jackson's 2nd grade class are studying communities. Right now, they are examining ways in which animal communities are like and unlike human communities. Last week, students viewed a video about ants. Yesterday, they read about bees and individually selected one other animal to learn about from a list Mr. Jackson provided. Today, as they proceed with their study, Mr. Jackson makes sure his students understand the elements of a community and how they might apply to animals. To help his students think about and make sense of these ideas, he uses cubing. Each six-sided cube carries these instructions for students: describe, compare, tell your feelings about, tell the parts of, use, and tell the good and bad things about.

Mr. Jackson assigned each student either a blue or green cube. Students using blue cubes are performing at or below grade level in reading and writing. Blue cube tasks are to

1. Describe an ant community in pictures or words.

2. Compare an ant community to your community in pictures or words.

3. List words that describe your feelings about watching an ant community.

4. Tell the parts of an ant community and what goes on in each part by using words or pictures or by building it.

5. Tell a way that an ant community helps you understand living and working together in a community.

6. Tell the good and bad things about an ant community.

Students using *green cubes* are performing above or well above grade level in reading and writing. Green cube tasks are to

1. Describe an ant community using at least three sentences with at least three describing words in each sentence.

2. Use a Venn diagram to compare an ant community with the community of the animal you selected.

3. Pretend that ants think like people. Write and cartoon what you think an ant feels like as it goes through a day in its community. Do the same thing with another kind of animal from a different sort of community.

4. Make a diagram of an animal community with parts labeled and tell what each part is for.

5. Write a rule for living together in a community and tell how it would be useful in two different communities.

6. Write a song or draw a picture that tells what you think is best and worst about being part of a community.

Students begin cubing by sitting at a table with other students using cubes of the same color. Students take turns rolling their cube. If the first roll turns up a task the student doesn't want to do, a second roll is allowed. As they work on their own task, students can also help one another. When their tasks are complete, Mr. Jackson rearranges the seating so that groups of four to five students who did a same-colored cube task can share with each other their varied ideas and approaches on a similar topic.

Blue cube tasks help learners think in a variety of ways about how key elements of community apply to a single animal community. Green cube tasks help learners make such connections among several animal communities. Compared to the blue cube tasks, green cube tasks are more transformational, complex, multifaceted, and require greater leaps of insight and transfer. Later in the unit, students who completed blue cube tasks will complete some of the green cube tasks either in small groups or by working directly with Mr. Jackson. Thus, all students engage in idea and information processing activities that not only match their learning profiles and current needs but also coax them forward on many learning continuums.

❦ ❦ ❦

Mrs. Miller and Interactive Journals

Mrs. Miller's 6th graders are all reading the novel *Tuck Everlasting*. She knows that the book is difficult for some of her students and doesn't much stretch some others, but she likes to have the class read some books together, just as she sometimes finds it useful to have several different novels read by her students simultaneously. Because the current novel is not a "best fit" for all learners in her class, she is making a special effort to ensure that she uses a differentiated process strategy that she does vary according to the student's readiness and interest.

By using differentiated interactive journals throughout this novel, Mrs. Miller provides her students with writing prompts that, for example, may encourage them to interact with the book as they predict what will occur next, reflect on something that has just taken place, apply understandings about elements of literature such as conflict or figurative language, relate to a character or situation, or grapple with meanings central to the authors' purposes in writing the book.

In the past, Mrs. Miller has given all students the same interactive journal prompts. This year, in trying to craft a differentiated classroom, some days she gives varied journal prompts to her students based on their interests and needs. On other days, all students will have the same prompt because it is essential for all of them to think about a common idea.

On the day prior to beginning the novel, she asks students to jot down what they think the word "everlasting" means. Based on those responses, as well as her cumulative knowledge about the students, she gives three different journal prompts on the next day as class begins. Students who seem unfamiliar with the word work in pairs to do the following:

1. Guess what "everlasting" means and write their "best guess" explanation.

2. Find definitions of the word in two dictionaries and use what they learn from the dictionary to write a good 6th grade definition of the word.

3. Write a definition of "everlasting" that would be crystal clear to a 1st grader.

4. Illustrate at least five things that they believe are everlasting, including defending why they think so.

5. Hypothesize what they think a book called *Tuck Everlasting* might be about.

A larger group of students who seemed to understand the word in the brief pre-assessment activity but whose general vocabulary and comprehension are generally within the expected range for 6th graders work either alone or with a partner on these tasks:

1. Hypothesize what a book called *Tuck Everlasting* might be about and explain how they came to their hypothesis.

2. Present and defend their choices of what sorts of things would be included as everlasting in a book written about everlasting things in their own lifetimes.

3. Present and defend their choices of what sorts of things would be included as everlasting in a book written about life 200 years ago.

4. Present and defend their choices of what sorts of things would be included as everlasting in a book written about life 200 years into the future.

Finally, a small group of students with advanced skills of vocabulary, writing, and abstraction work together as a group to do the following:

1. Place on a continuum of "less enduring" to "more enduring" a list of items such as gold, coal, love, friendship, energy, time, fear, happiness, and additional items of their choosing.

2. Write a poem or paragraph that expresses their reasoning in placing the items on the continuum.

3. Hypothesize what a book called *Tuck Everlasting* might be about and be ready to defend their hypothesis.

All students in the class use interactive journals and have a task that causes them to make leaps of thought and insight and to deal with a powerful and central concept in the book they are about to begin reading together. These three interactive journal assignments themselves, however, are increasingly transformational, abstract, open-ended, and require increasingly greater leaps of thought for successful completion.

When class starts on the day they begin the novel, Mrs. Miller accommodates her students' varied pacing needs by distributing their journal assignment sheets, giving the instruction to read at least the first 25 pages of the novel, and then letting them be free to work as long as necessary in class on the journal prompt and complete the rest at home that night. This attention to pacing allows each student to work at a comfortable pace; ensures that all students have adequate, purposeful work to do during the class period; and offers enough time so that all should be prepared for a short, whole-class discussion at the beginning of class on day two of the novel unit.

❦ ❦ ❦

Sense-making strategies help students process and "own" ideas and information in ways that work best for them. The next chapter on differentiating products describes strategies that allow students to demonstrate—again, in ways that work best for them—the results of all that processing.

Differentiating Products

Unlike a sense-making activity, which is typically short and focuses on one, or just a few, key understandings and skills, a product is a long-term endeavor. Product assignments should help students—individually or in groups—rethink, use, and extend what they have learned over a long period of time—a unit, a semester, or even a year. Products are important not only because they represent your students' extensive understandings and applications, but also because they are the element of curriculum students can most directly "own." For that reason, well-designed product assignments can be highly motivating because they will bear their creator's thumbprint.

High-quality product assignments are also excellent ways of assessing student knowledge, understanding, and skill. Many students can show what they know far better in a product than on a written test. Therefore, in a differenti-

ated classroom, teachers may replace some tests with rich product assignments, or combine tests and product options so the broadest range of students has maximum opportunity to think about, apply, and demonstrate what they have learned.

Creating High-Quality Product Assignments

A teacher crafts a top-rate product assignment with thought and care. A good product is not just something students do for enjoyment at the end of a unit. It must cause students to think about, apply, and even expand on all the key understandings and skills of the learning span it represents.

Once a teacher is clear on the knowledge, understandings, and skills the product must incorporate, it's time to decide on what format the product will take. Sometimes the format is a given because of requirements of a curriculum (e.g., writing an essay, designing an experiment, and so on). Often, however, the teacher can use a product as a way to lure students into application of ideas and skills (e.g., using photography as a way to hook young adolescents on poetry). Sometimes a teacher can use a product assignment as a way to help students explore modes of expression unfamiliar to them (e.g., learning to create a museum exhibit, conduct a symposium, or develop a journal article as ways of helping students see how scientists communicate what they know). The very best product formats may be those with which students have a love affair at a given time (e.g., a 3rd grader, who was talented in music, wrote a musical to share information and understandings about the westward movement in the United States).

Then it's important for the teacher to determine core expectations for quality students to pursue in regard to the content in their products, how they should work on their products, and the nature of the final product itself. Students can add to and help the teacher modify the core requirements to address individual readiness, interests, and learning needs, but it is the teacher's job to know and communicate indicators of quality. Students seldom know how to extend their vision in pursuit of quality without help from adults or more expert-like peers.

Because the product assignment should stretch students in application of understanding and skill as well as in pursuit of quality, a teacher needs to determine ways in which she can assist the student in reaching a new level of possibility as the product assignment progresses. This sort of scaffolding allows students to find success at the end of hard work rather than overdoses of confusion and ambiguity. Teachers may arrange times for brainstorming ideas to launch the product, for workshops on conducting research or synthesizing findings, for setting and assessing personal product goals, for peer consultation and editing, for actual product design, and so on. The goal is to antici-

pate what is necessary to lift the student's sights and build bridges to attaining lofty goals.

Finally, it's time for the teacher to present the product assignment (in writing, orally, on tape, with icons, through models, or with some combination of these). The assignment should make clear to students what knowledge, understanding, and skills they must include in their work; the stages, processes, and work habits they should demonstrate as they work; the option(s) for expressing their learning; and what quality will look like. Within this structure, there should still be maximum room for individual interests, modes of working, personal quality goals, and so on. The trick is to balance the structure needed to focus and guide students, and the freedom necessary to support innovation and thought.

Only at this point does it become time to differentiate the product assignment. Teachers and students can make adaptations of the core product according to student readiness, interest, and learning profile. Some teachers also like to have a "let's make a deal" product choice through which students can propose alternatives to the teacher's design, as long as the alternative leads students to grapple with key information, understandings, and skills that are at the essence of the assignment's purpose.

It's really helpful for a teacher to coach for quality throughout the product span. Invite students to talk about their ideas, progress, glitches, ways of solving problems, and so on. Share your own excitement about their ideas. Clarify what quality means. Talk about how successful people work. Build a sense of personal ownership of work as well as group appreciation of the varied approaches and ideas of members of the group.

Figure 13.1 (see next page) summarizes components of effective product design, including the differentiation component. It's always important to remember that good differentiated curriculum and instruction—whether content,

Figure 13.1
Creating a Powerful Product Assignment

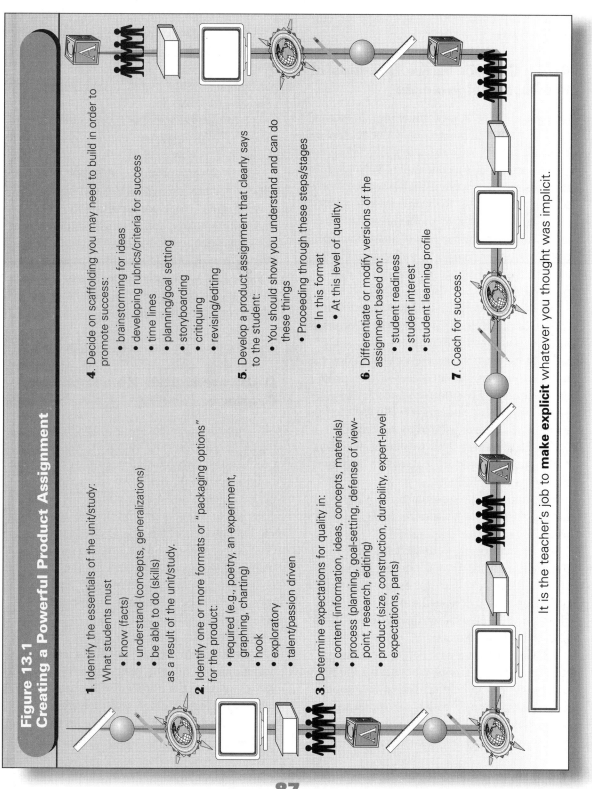

1. Identify the essentials of the unit/study:
   What students must
   - know (facts)
   - understand (concepts, generalizations)
   - be able to do (skills)
   as a result of the unit/study.

2. Identify one or more formats or "packaging options" for the product:
   - required (e.g., poetry, an experiment, graphing, charting)
   - hook
   - exploratory
   - talent/passion driven

3. Determine expectations for quality in:
   - content (information, ideas, concepts, materials)
   - process (planning, goal-setting, defense of view-point, research, editing)
   - product (size, construction, durability, expert-level expectations, parts)

4. Decide on scaffolding you may need to build in order to promote success:
   - brainstorming for ideas
   - developing rubrics/criteria for success
   - time lines
   - planning/goal setting
   - storyboarding
   - critiquing
   - revising/editing

5. Develop a product assignment that clearly says to the student:
   - You should show you understand and can do these things
   - Proceeding through these steps/stages
     - In this format
       - At this level of quality.

6. Differentiate or modify versions of the assignment based on:
   - student readiness
   - student interest
   - student learning profile

7. Coach for success.

It is the teacher's job to **make explicit** whatever you thought was implicit.

process, or product—first have to be good curriculum and instruction.

Other Guidelines for Successful Product Assignments

Here are a few additional guidelines to maximize the power of product assignments and to build for student success:

1. Use products as one way to help your students see the ideas and skills they study in school being used in the world by real people to address real issues or problems.

2. Talk with your students often about the need for both critical and creative thinking. Help them build a passion for ideas being pursued.

3. Require that your students use and synthesize or blend multiple sources of information in developing their products.

4. Stress planning and use check-in dates as needed to match students' levels of independence. Zap procrastination.

5. Ensure that students actually use the entire block of time allotted to the project (rather than waiting three weeks and five days of a monthlong product span before beginning to work on the product).

6. Support your students' use of varied modes of expression, materials, and technologies.

7. Be sure to help your students learn required production skills, not just necessary content. Don't ask them, for example, to do a debate or teach a class without giving them clear guidance on what quality would look like in each of those formats.

8. Communicate with parents regarding time lines, requirements, rationale for the product, how they can help, and what they should avoid doing during creation of the product.

9. Remember that there are many ways people can express themselves. Help students get

out of the poster-report-mobile rut of products. Figure 13.2 lists just some of the possibilities.

10. Use formative (during the project) and summative (after the project) peer and self-evaluation based on the agreed-upon criteria for content and production.

11. Whenever possible, arrange for student products to be viewed by someone other than just you.

12. In sharing products, remember that having every student share with the whole class may be unduly time-consuming—and even uninspiring, unless you've taught students how to be high-quality presenters. Using exhibits, sharing groups of four, individual presentations to key adults who serve as mentors or audiences, and so on can be great alternatives to whole-class presentations.

❦ ❦ ❦

A Differentiated Kindergarten Product

Mrs. Appleton's kindergartners have been studying neighborhoods and communities. As a final product, they are going to research, design, and build a portion of their town, showing its neighborhoods and communities. The whole class is working as a group to create and share the final model, which will be quite large. The class will make some decisions and do some tasks as a whole, such as deciding the basic contents of the model and making "blank buildings" that will be turned into representations of actual buildings later.

Students will select other facets of the work based on their interests: Everyone selects one community member to interview as a way of gathering data, some students have selected to make signs for buildings, and each student selects a neighborhood to work on in the model.

Figure 13.2
Product Possibilities

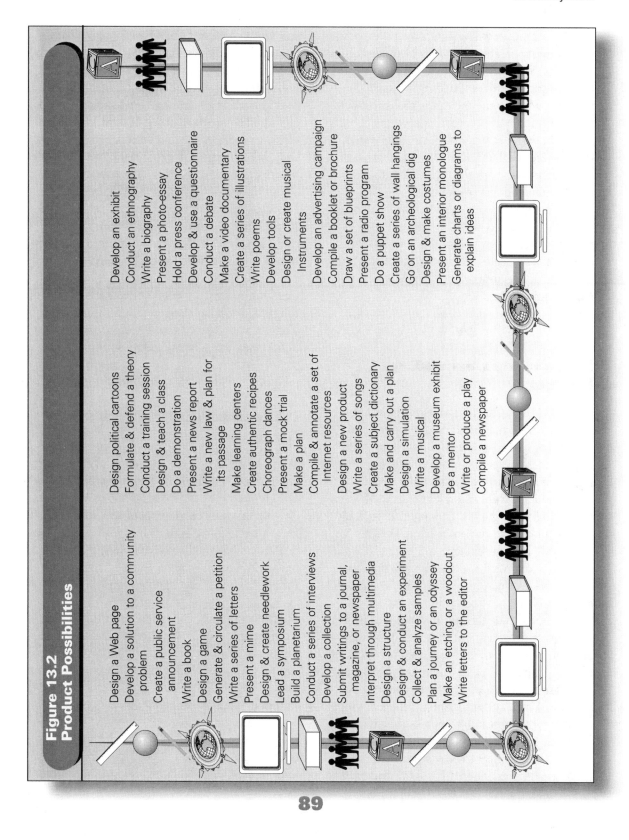

Design a Web page
Develop a solution to a community problem
Create a public service announcement
Write a book
Design a game
Generate & circulate a petition
Write a series of letters
Present a mime
Design & create needlework
Lead a symposium
Build a planetarium
Conduct a series of interviews
Develop a collection
Submit writings to a journal, magazine, or newspaper
Interpret through multimedia
Design a structure
Design & conduct an experiment
Collect & analyze samples
Plan a journey or an odyssey
Make an etching or a woodcut
Write letters to the editor

Design political cartoons
Formulate & defend a theory
Conduct a training session
Design & teach a class
Do a demonstration
Present a news report
Write a new law & plan for its passage
Make learning centers
Create authentic recipes
Choreograph dances
Present a mock trial
Make a plan
Compile & annotate a set of Internet resources
Design a new product
Write a series of songs
Create a subject dictionary
Make and carry out a plan
Design a simulation
Write a musical
Develop a museum exhibit
Be a mentor
Write or produce a play
Compile a newspaper

Develop an exhibit
Conduct an ethnography
Write a biography
Present a photo-essay
Hold a press conference
Develop & use a questionnaire
Conduct a debate
Make a video documentary
Create a series of illustrations
Write poems
Develop tools
Design or create musical Instruments
Develop an advertising campaign
Compile a booklet or brochure
Draw a set of blueprints
Present a radio program
Do a puppet show
Create a series of wall hangings
Go on an archeological dig
Design & make costumes
Present an interior monologue
Generate charts or diagrams to explain ideas

Mrs. Appleton will assign some tasks, however, to draw on and extend each student's strengths. Students more skilled with measuring will measure and draw building dimensions. Students with strong fine motor skills will cut some of the complex pieces, and others not so skilled in that area will assemble some of the larger pieces of the model. Mrs. Appleton will ask students who are already reading to look up information and help make signs.

She carefully designed this project to ensure that all students do both self-selected and teacher-selected (readiness-based) tasks. Mrs. Appleton also makes sure that some tasks require students to work collegially, while other tasks require independent work.

❦ ❦ ❦

Differentiated Secondary Products

Students in Mr. Garcia's Spanish II class are working on language and culture projects. A goal for all his students is to understand more fully how elements of a given culture interrelate and form a distinct personality of a people. Many students will explore the culture of Spain by writing travel guides, making videos, filming documentaries, or presenting dramas. They will investigate history, religion, economics, celebrations, geography, education, climate, literature, art, language structure, and how those elements are interrelated.

Although students have a number of product requirements laid out for them, they will add some of their own criteria for success. They also can choose whether to work alone or in a small group, which mode of expression they will use, which cultural elements they will focus on, and which research resources they will use.

Three students in the class are quite advanced in their grasp of Spanish because language is a high talent area for them; and for two

students, Spanish is their first language. Mr. Garcia wants these three students to work with the same concepts as the other students in the class—but to stretch their thinking, he will differentiate their assignment and ask them to do cross-cultural comparisons. They will examine elements of language and culture across at least three language groups other than Spanish, none of which can be a modern Romance language. These students will examine languages such as Swahili, Farsi, Chinese, Japanese, Hebrew, and Russian, as well as the cultures from which those languages arise. These advanced students have a bit more freedom in designing their final products and the processes for reaching their final destinations. And like the other students in the class, they can also select whether to work alone or with peers and the form through which they will express their learning.

❦ ❦ ❦

Differentiating Products for Struggling Learners

We often expect far too little of struggling learners. Product assignments are a great place to stretch our sights for students and to help them develop confidence as learners and producers. Here are some suggestions for ensuring that students who have difficulty with school tasks have both challenging products to create and support systems leading to success.

1. Be sure product assignments for all learners require them to apply and extend essential understandings and skills for the unit or other product span. (Integrate skills and other goals from individualized educational plans [IEPs] into rich product formats.)

2. Use product formats that allow students to express themselves in ways other than written language alone.

3. Give product assignments in smaller increments, allowing students to complete one portion of a product before introducing another.

5. Think about putting directions on audio or video tape so students can revisit explanations as needed.

6. Prepare, or help students prepare, time lines for product work so that tasks seem manageable and comfortably structured.

7. Use miniworkshops on particular product skills such as taking notes in research, conducting interviews, drawing conclusions, editing, and so on. Many students will benefit from options to attend such miniworkshops, including some students who struggle academically.

8. Support students in finding appropriate resources by setting up interviews, bookmarking Internet sites, creating special book boxes or shelves of readable sources on related topics, tape-recording summaries of key ideas and information, enlisting media specialists to work with students at established times, and so on.

9. Provide templates or organizers that guide students through each step of doing research.

10. From time to time be sure to review the big picture of the product with the students—asking them to reflect on why it's important, what they are learning, how parts of the product fit together to make a big picture of meaning, how the product relates to what's going on in class, and so on.

11. Where students find tasks daunting think about joining (or having specialists join) individuals or groups in an ad hoc, advisory capacity—meeting at pre-established times for consultation, coaching, and guidance.

12. Work with students to target portions of rubrics that reflect their individual needs, focusing both yourself and students on goals that seem challenging and worthwhile for particular emphasis.

13. Help students analyze models of effective products from prior years so that they develop awareness of important components of

the product, language skills to think about the elements, and concrete illustrations of what good work looks like.

14. When students do not have resources and support for product completion outside of school, provide time, materials, and partnership at school. This may take place before or after school, during class, during released time from class, at lunch, or even on weekends. It's important for every student to have an adult support system that speaks of belief in the student and investment in making sure the belief becomes reality.

15. When students speak a primary language other than English, be sure the student has access to information in his first language, or a strong support system for translating. Also, think about including a stage in the time line to allow students initially to express ideas in their first language and then to translate them (with appropriate assistance) into English.

Differentiating Product Assignments for Advanced Learners

As is the case with content and process, the idea with product design for advanced learners is to ensure that learners actually have to stretch their information base, understanding, thought processes, planning and production skills, and self-awareness. Product assignments that are quite challenging in these ways for many students often fall short of a genuine challenge for students highly able in a given subject. Moving the "equalizer buttons" (see Figure 8.1, page 47) over toward the right as you modify product assignments for these learners is your goal. Here are a few principles useful for adapting product assignments for advanced learners.

1. Be sure to structure product assignments for advanced learners so that they're being stretched forward on a number of the learning

continuums—complexity, independence, transformation, abstractness, multifaceted solutions, and great leaps of insight.

2. Consider having advanced learners study the key issues or questions across time periods, disciplines, or cultures.

3. As much as possible, include advanced-level research, such as advanced materials, multiple materials, primary sources, original documents, and student-conducted original research.

4. Consider using mentors to guide the work of advanced learners so that the students are stretched in content and quality by someone who knows the area of study at an advanced level.

5. Consider letting advanced students begin their projects earlier than other students if the complexity of their products warrants it. Working on their products might then become an ongoing assignment when they compact out of classwork and when they do not need to do the homework practice important for other learners.

6. Whenever possible, have each advanced learner work with a mentor—someone who works avocationally or professionally with the topic being explored.

7. Let each advanced learner help you develop criteria for expert-level content and production. Work together to determine issues that experts would feel must be dealt with in the product exploration, ways in which those issues should be dealt with, and procedures and standards for production that would be important to an expert. Use these as benchmarks for student planning and assessment.

8. When it would be helpful to do so, have advanced learners' products assessed by an expert in the field on which the product is based. In some instances, expert assessment is most helpful at a *formative* or in-process stage of work so that the student can clarify and extend ideas prior to completion of the product. In other instances, *summative* or end-stage assessment by an expert is useful for advanced learners who want to test their product against genuine high standards. It is often the case that teachers lack some of the knowledge and skills of a professional in a given area of study. Helping advanced learners gain access to those skills and understandings is an important way of ensuring that they stretch their capacity instead of continuing to be rewarded for "doing what comes naturally."

Final Thoughts on Differentiating Products for All Learners

The ways to design, support, and assess challenging product assignments are endless. Just remember to provide written guidelines, which may be lengthy at times, so students have adequate structure, challenge, and clarity of purpose and expectations.

Differentiating product assignments in a mixed-ability classroom is beneficial for several reasons. If all products relate to the same key information and understandings, then all students can share in conversations among individuals, small groups, and the whole class. This can occur even as students work in ways that address their *own* readiness levels, interests, and learning modes. By offering variations on well-designed products with core commonalities, teachers encourage all students to draw on their personal interests and strengths. In these ways, all students can grow from appropriate challenges. At the same time, the teacher retains focus on those curricular components he or she deems essential to all learners.

🐾 🐾 🐾

The next chapter takes a close look at grading, with a focus on student performance and parent involvement.

Grading **IN A** Differentiated Classroom

14

By now, it should be clear that in a differentiated classroom, students often work at different paces and are assessed according to varied learning goals. Two important features of a differentiated classroom are students' rights to "begin where they are" and to expect to grow as learners. But charting and acknowledging the academic growth of individual students in a differentiated classroom can create a dilemma for teachers whose schools still use a traditional report card and grading system.

On the one hand, the public expects "normed" report cards. On the other hand, ample evidence indicates that traditional grades may not communicate or motivate as we would like to believe they do (Ornstein, 1994). Here are four approaches to this problem that have proved useful.

Changing the Traditional Grading System

Before doing away with a traditional grading system, some teachers and schools have found that it's important to explain to students and their parents how the new system will work. Students and parents learn that the new grading system is based on individual goal setting and progress in reaching those goals, and that students will be "graded against themselves" rather than in competition with other students. Portfolio-type assessment and reporting of progress work well in such settings.

Other teachers and schools choose to combine traditional letter grades on report cards with an additional piece of information. The report card carries the information that an *A* still means excellent performance, a *B* means good performance, and so on. But each letter grade now also carries a numeric "superscript":

a *1* means working above grade level, a *2* means working at grade level, and a *3* means working below grade level. Thus, students who achieve an A[3] are clearly working hard and progressing well, even though their work is not yet at grade-level norms. A report card using this grading system probably offers more information than a traditional report card.

Another approach is to give two grades—a personal one and a "traditional" one. Thus, a struggling learner might receive a *B* on progress toward reaching personal learner goals and a *D* when compared with the class. An advanced learner who is not "pushing his own ceiling" might get a *C* in progress toward personal goals and an *A* in comparison with the rest of the class. When using this type of system, it is important to help parents and students clearly understand the utility of each piece of information in educational planning.

Finally, some educators urge teachers to routinely share varied sorts of information with parents and students, such as personal grades or portfolios that help everyone see and understand a student's progress, grades or other information that shows how a student compares with classmates, and nationally normed data that may give a picture of that student compared with a still larger group (Gilman & McDermott, 1994). Again, parent education and partnership are important in such instances.

In the best of worlds, the first alternative has much to commend it. In the real world, any system that encourages personal growth in every student should be the goal and may be achieved, at least in part, in a variety of ways.

Handling Concerns of Advanced Learners and Their Parents

When switching to a grading system where students compete against themselves, the learners most likely to encounter initial difficulty are high-ability students who have not had to work

hard to get good grades. Sometimes it takes a while for these students to develop work habits and standards that challenge their abilities. During this transition time, their grades on tests, projects, or report cards may be lower than they and their parents are accustomed to. In such cases, it is critical that you help both students and parents understand the value of teaching children to "reach high."

Unfortunately, many high-ability learners don't encounter a real challenge until they take an advanced high school course or get to college. The first time they meet failure—or something other than predictable success—they may panic. Their self-esteem can be greatly diminished or completely destroyed. They often remove themselves from the situation in frustration and fear. Even if they do try to meet the challenge, they frequently find they have no sense of how to study or to monitor and improve their own effectiveness as a problem solver. For several reasons, teachers do such students a real favor by helping them encounter and face challenges when they are younger. Parents and teachers are usually more available to help students at an earlier age. Not so much is at stake yet in the way of grades and futures. And most important, learning to face challenges earlier gives these students more time to develop the planning, self-evaluation, and study skills they need to maximize their potential as learners.

If high-ability students and their parents panic at the onset of challenge, you can be a voice of calm and reason. Encourage parents to work with you in helping their children reach up for challenge rather than running from it.

Record-Keeping in a Differentiated Classroom

Developing classrooms in which students engage in varied content, sense-making activities, and product execution often requires teachers to modify their more traditional ways of keeping track of student growth. Although teachers employ many useful strategies to chart student tasks and growth, it is important to recall that the dual purpose of all assessment is (1) to chart student growth in regard to valued skills and knowledge and (2) to use information gathered through that process to help in planning the most appropriate learning experiences possible for given individuals and groups of students. Guidelines presented here may help you begin to develop a record-keeping system that works best for you, the nature of your classroom, and the age of your learners.

1. You don't have to throw out your grade book! Often, just relabeling the columns in a less-specific and more-generic way will be adequate. In an arithmetic class where all students complete the *same* activity for a grade on a given day, the heading over the grade column might say *Ex. p. 211* to reflect that the grades below are on the fraction exercise found on page 211 of the text. In a class where students of varied readiness levels complete a variety of sense-making activities on fractions, your heading might read *Fract/4-9*, indicating that the grades below are on whatever assignment a student completed on April 9 related to fractions. A quick reference list of assignments, students working with them, and dates would enable you to look at the April 9 heading and reference which assignment Bobby, for example, worked on that day. Or you might elect to label a grade book column with the key concept or principle being explored by students. A grade in that column, then, would indicate to you that a particular student made a given grade on the activity appropriate for her related to that concept.

2. Student work folders are a valuable record-keeping device. Regardless of the age of your students, having them maintain a folder that keeps a running record of work completed, dates of completion, student or teacher comments about the work, and work samples is a powerful record-keeping aid. Color-coded folders for each period of the day can make distribution, collection, and storage of folders easy. Student work folders should contain record-keeping forms (e.g., student-choice reading lists, spelling lists, skills proficiencies demonstrated, product assignments, and others), samples of student work, records of conferences with the teacher, student goals, and other data that would help both student and teacher maintain a sense of focus and direction. Use of these folders is also a powerful tool during planning conferences with students and parent-teacher conferences that focus on student growth. It won't take you long to discover that it's necessary to allot a few minutes every few weeks for folder clean out.

3. Share as much record-keeping responsibility as possible with your students. Even very young learners can keep a calendar of daily or weekly activities, maintain records of reading, record their progress at a center or station by using forms left at those workplaces, and select work that they feel shows best what they have learned. Students can hand out and collect folders, prepare portfolios for parent conferences, write reports or use checklists to show their progress to parents and teachers, and assume responsibility for a myriad of other procedures that make record-keeping less demanding on you the teacher. Students who serve as an "expert of the day" can often check in work, monitor accuracy of completion of tasks, or make a record of which students have worked on a given task at a given time. Helping students become effective record-keepers also helps them develop clarity regarding goals, assignments and their progress; assists them in metacognition or thinking about what goes on around them in the classroom; and provides them with skills of organization that serve them well in many settings.

4. Consider the possibility that not all work has to be formally graded. An athlete may practice shooting 3-point baskets for many days. Formal "assessment" of his progress and skill comes days or weeks later in a game when he has a chance to apply what he has learned. A young musician goes to a violin lesson where the teacher explains and demonstrates what is required in order to grow in proficiency with the instrument. The youngster goes home to practice those skills for a week, returns for another cycle of advice and affirmation the next week, practices again, and undergoes formal assessment weeks or months later in a recital. No one feels the need to grade each basket-shooting session or each half hour of violin practice.

Similarly, sense-making activities need not be formally graded each day. A well-constructed product assignment or test should provide adequate evidence of what the student knows and can do. A teacher who practices this principle may make daily jottings on a clipboard (which she carries around during her interactions with students) or in a grade book to note who is or is not engaged in their work, questions students ask, points of difficulty and clarity for varied students, and so forth, in lieu of formally correcting and grading all sense-making activities. This information can be used to develop upcoming assignments for students based on observed needs and strengths.

Simultaneously, such a teacher facilitates intellectual risk taking in students who do not have to fear making mistakes, but who learn that life typically offers opportunity to gain a skill before judging us on that skill. A student in this class can also complete assignments at an appropriate pace, because it is not necessary that all learners have the same number of grades in the grade book. What matters more is that all students have had an appropriate number of opportunities (ranging from zero to many) to make sense of and demonstrate their ability to apply concepts, principles, skills, and information related to a given area of study.

5. Involve students in student-led parent conferences. Asking students to be a part of goalsetting with you, to keep track of their work and how it demonstrates their growth, and to communicate this information to parents can be powerful for everyone. It helps students develop responsibility for and a voice about their own work. It helps you and parents hear the same student messages about what's working and what isn't. It makes much clearer than you can alone why it matters to have work that matches student needs. It also addresses the reality that learning itself is learned, and that students who have cooperative teacher-parent partners in finding an optimum learning match are fortunate indeed.

ᴀ Final Thought

Fourten-year-old Kathleen wrote a poem a number of years ago. She was a high-ability learner who seldom found a serious reason to extend her academic reach in school. Then she encountered a teacher who caused her to find new power in herself. At the end of that school year, Kathleen wrote a poem to her teacher. On some level, it expresses the need of all students—and all humans—to push their own limits. It certainly describes Kathleen's acknowledgement of what it was like for her when that need was fulfilled. Her words also seem to express her clear sense of the role her teacher had played in that magical year, as the teacher saw Kathleen and dealt with her as an individual.

Push me! See how far I go!
Work me 'til I drop. Then pick me up.
Open a door, and then make me run to
    it before it closes.
Teach me so that I might learn,
Then let me enter the tunnel of
    experience alone.
And when, near the end,
I turn to see you beginning another's
    journey,
I shall smile.

HOW TO Differentiate Instruction IN Mixed-Ability Classrooms

A Few Instructional and Management Strategies for Differentiated, Mixed-Ability Classrooms

STRATEGY	DESCRIPTION OF STRATEGY	RATIONALE FOR USE	GUIDELINES FOR USE
Compacting	A 3-step process that (1) assesses what a student knows about material to be studied and what the student still needs to master, (2) plans for learning what is not known and excuses student from what is known, and (3) plans for freed-up time to be spent in enriched or accelerated study.	• Recognizes large reservoir of knowledge in some learners • Satisfies hunger to learn more about more topics than school often allows • Encourages independence • Eliminates boredom and lethargy resulting from unnecessary drill and practice	• Explain the process and its benefits to students and parents • Pre-assess learner's knowledge and documents findings • Allow student much choice in use of time "bought" through previous mastery • Use written plans and time lines for accelerated or enrichment study • Can use group compacting for several students

(continued on next page)

A Few Instructional and Management Strategies
for Differentiated, Mixed-Ability Classrooms—continued

STRATEGY	DESCRIPTION OF STRATEGY	RATIONALE FOR USE	GUIDELINES FOR USE
Independent Projects	A process through which student and teacher identify problems or topics of interest to the student. Both student and teacher plan a method of investigating the problem or topic and identifying the type of product the student will develop. This product should address the problem and demonstrate the student's ability to apply skills and knowledge to the problem or topic.	• Builds on student interest • Satisfies curiosity • Teaches planning and research skills at advanced levels • Encourages independence • Allows work with complex and abstract ideas • Allows long-term and in-depth work on topics of interest • Taps into high motivation	• Build on student interest • Allow the student maximum freedom to plan, *based on student readiness for freedom* • Teacher provides guidance and structure to supplement student capacity to plan and to ensure high standards of production • Use preset time lines to zap procrastination • Use process logs to document the process involved throughout the study • Establish criteria for success

(continued on next page)

A Few Instructional and Management Strategies for Differentiated, Mixed-Ability Classrooms—continued

STRATEGY	DESCRIPTION OF STRATEGY	RATIONALE FOR USE	GUIDELINES FOR USE
Interest Centers or Interest Groups	Interest centers (often used with younger learners) and interest groups (often used with older learners) can provide enrichment for students who demonstrate mastery/competence with required work and can be a vehicle for providing these students with meaningful study when required assignments are completed. In addition, all learners enjoy and need the opportunity to work with interest centers/groups in order to pursue areas of special interest to them. These centers/groups can be differentiated by level of complexity and independence required, as well as by student interest, to make them accessible and appropriately challenging for all learners.	• Allows student choice • Taps into student interest—motivating • Satisfies curiosity—explores hows and whys • Allows study of topics not in the regular curriculum • Can allow for study in greater breadth and depth • Can be modified for student readiness • Can encourage students to make connections between fields of study or between study and life	• Build on student interest • Encourage students to help you develop interest-based tasks • Adjust for student readiness • Allow students of like interests to work together • Develop clear (differentiated) criteria for success • For advanced learners, allow long blocks of time for work, change centers less often to allow for depth of study, make certain tasks are challenging

(continued on next page)

Appendix – continued

A Few Instructional and Management Strategies for Differentiated, Mixed-Ability Classrooms—continued

STRATEGY	DESCRIPTION OF STRATEGY	RATIONALE FOR USE	GUIDELINES FOR USE
Tiered Assignments	In a heterogeneous classroom, a teacher uses varied levels of activities to ensure that students explore ideas at a level that builds on their prior knowledge and prompts continued growth. Student groups use varied approaches to exploration of essential ideas.	• Blends assessment and instruction • Allows students to begin learning from where they are • Allows students to work with appropriately challenging tasks • Allows for reinforcement or extension of concepts and principles based on student readiness • Allows modification of working conditions based on learning style • Avoids work that is anxiety-producing (too hard) or boredom-producing (too easy) • Promotes success and is therefore motivating	• Be sure the task is focused on a key concept or generalization essential to the study • Use a variety of resource materials at differing levels of complexity and associated with different learning modes • Adjust the task by complexity, abstractness, number of steps, concreteness, and independence to ensure appropriate challenge • Be certain there are clear criteria for quality and success

(continued on next page)

101

Appendix – continued

A Few Instructional and Management Strategies for Differentiated, Mixed-Ability Classrooms—continued

STRATEGY	DESCRIPTION OF STRATEGY	RATIONALE FOR USE	GUIDELINES FOR USE
Flexible Grouping	Students are part of many different groups—and also work alone—based on the match of the task to student readiness, interest, or learning style. Teachers may create skills-based or interest-based groups that are heterogeneous or homogeneous in readiness level. Sometimes students select work groups, and sometimes teachers select them. Sometimes student group assignments are purposeful and sometimes random.	• Allows both for quick mastery of information/ideas and need for additional exploration by students needing more time for mastery • Allows both collaborative and independent work • Gives students and teachers a voice in work arrangements • Allows students to work with a wide variety of peers • Encourages teachers to "try out" students in a variety of work settings • Keeps students from being "pegged" as advanced or struggling • Keeps students from being cast as those in need of help and those who are helpers	• Ensure that all students have opportunities to work both with students most like themselves and with students dissimilar from themselves in readiness and interest • Teacher assigns work groups when task is designed to match individual readiness/interest based on pre-assessment or teacher knowledge • Teacher assigns work groups when desirable to ensure that students work with a variety of classmates • Students select groups when task is well-suited for peer selection • Alternate purposeful assignment to groups with teacher/student selection • Ensure that all students learn to work cooperatively, collaboratively, and independently • Be sure there are clear guidelines for group functioning that are taught in advance of group work and consistently reinforced

(continued on next page)

Appendix – continued

AA Few Instructional and Management Strategies for Differentiated, Mixed-Ability Classrooms—continued

STRATEGY	DESCRIPTION OF STRATEGY	RATIONALE FOR USE	GUIDELINES FOR USE
Learning Centers	Learning centers can be "stations" or collections of materials learners use to explore topics or practice skills. Teachers can adjust learning center tasks to readiness levels or learning styles of different students.	• Allows matching task with learner's skills level • Encourages continuous development of student skills • Allows matching task with student learning style • Enables students to work at appropriate pace • Allows teacher to break class into practice and direct instruction groups at a given time • Helps develop student independence	• Match task to learner readiness, interest, learning style • Avoid having all learners do all work at all centers • Teach students to record their own progress at centers • Monitor what students do and what they understand at centers • Have clear directions and clear criteria for success at centers

(continued on next page)

Appendix – continued

A Few Instructional and Management Strategies for Differentiated, Mixed-Ability Classrooms—continued

STRATEGY	DESCRIPTION OF STRATEGY	RATIONALE FOR USE	GUIDELINES FOR USE
Varying Questions	In class discussions and on tests, teachers vary the sorts of questions posed to learners based on their readiness, interests, and learning styles.	• All students need to be accountable for information and thinking at high levels • Some students will be challenged by a more basic thought question • Others will be challenged by a question that requires speed of response, large leaps of insight, or making remote connections • Teachers can "try out" students with varied sorts of questions as one means of assessing student progress and readiness • Varying questions appropriately helps nurture motivation through success • In oral settings, all students can hear and learn from a wide range of responses	• Target some questions to particular students and "open the floor" to others • Use open-ended questions where possible • Use wait time before taking answers • When appropriate, give students a chance to talk with thinking partners before giving answers • Encourage students to build on one another's answers • Require students to explain and defend their answers • Adjust the complexity, abstractness, degree of mental leap required, time constraints, connections required between topics, and so forth, based on learning profile of the student being asked a question

(continued on next page)

Appendix – continued

A Few Instructional and Management Strategies for Differentiated, Mixed-Ability Classrooms—continued

STRATEGY	DESCRIPTION OF STRATEGY	RATIONALE FOR USE	GUIDELINES FOR USE
Mentorships/ Apprentice- ships	Students work with a resource teacher, media specialist, parent volunteer, older student, or community member who can guide their growth in a particular area. Some mentorships may focus on design and execution of advanced projects, some on exploration of particular work settings, and some on affective development, and some on combinations of goals.	• Mentorships extend learning beyond the classroom • Mentorships make learning a partnership • Mentorships can help students expand awareness of future options and how to attain them • Mentorships allow teachers to tap into student interest, strengths, and needs • Mentorships have a low teacher-to-learner ratio (often one-to-one)	• Match the mentor with the student's needs (interests, strengths, culture, gender) • Be clear in your own mind and specific about the goals of the collaboration • Make sure roles of mentor, student, teacher, and parent are written and agreed upon • Provide appropriate preparation and instruction for mentors, including key information about the student • Monitor the progress of the mentorship regularly and help problem solve if snags occur • Connect what is learned in the mentorship to what goes on in class whenever feasible

(continued on next page)

Appendix – continued

A Few Instructional and Management Strategies
for Differentiated, Mixed-Ability Classrooms—continued

STRATEGY	DESCRIPTION OF STRATEGY	RATIONALE FOR USE	GUIDELINES FOR USE
Contracts	Contracts take a number of forms that begin with an agreement between student and teacher: The teacher grants certain freedoms and choices about how a student will complete tasks, and the student agrees to use the freedoms appropriately in designing and completing work according to specifications.	• Can blend skill- and content-based learning matched to student's need • Eliminates unnecessary skill practice for students • Allows students to work at appropriate pace • Helps students learn planning and decision-making skills important for independence as learners • Allows teachers time to work with individuals and small groups • Can encourage extended study on topics of interest • Can foster research, critical and creative thinking, application of skills, and integrated learning	• Blend both skill- and content-based learning in the contract • Match skills to readiness of the learner • Match content to readiness, interests, and learning style of student • Allow student choice, especially in content-based portions of the contract • From the outset, establish clear and challenging standards for success • Provide rules for the contract in writing • When possible, focus the contract on concepts, themes, or problems, and integrate appropriate skills into required projects or products • Vary levels of student independence and time span of the contract to match student readiness

(continued on next page)

References

American Association of School Administrators. (1991). *Learning styles: Putting research and common sense into practice*. Arlington, VA: Author.

Bess, J. (1997). Teaching well and liking it: *Motivating faculty to teach effectively*. Baltimore, MD: The Johns Hopkins University Press.

Brandt, R. (1998). *Powerful learning*. Alexandria, VA: Association for Supervision and Curriculum Development.

Clark, B. (1992). *Growing up gifted*. New York: Macmillan.

Clarke, J. (1994). Pieces of the puzzle: The Jigsaw method. In S. Sharan (Ed.), *Handbook of cooperative learning methods* (pp. 34–50). Westport, CT: The Greenwood Press.

Cohen, E. (1994). Designing groupwork: *Strategies for the heterogeneous classroom* (2nd ed.). New York: Teachers College Press.

Daniels, H. (1994). *Literature circles: Voice and choice in the student-centered classroom*. York, ME: Stenhouse Publishers.

Delpit, L. (1995). *Other people's children: Cultural conflict in the classroom*. New York: The New Press.

Dewey, J. (1938). *Experience and education*. New York: Macmillan.

Dunn, R., Beaudry, J., & Klavas, A. (1989). *Survey of research on learning styles*. Educational Leadership, 46(6), 50–58.

Fountas, I., & Pinnell, G. (1996). *Guided reading: Good first teaching for all*. Portsmouth, NH: Heinemann.

Gardner, H. (1983). *Frames of mind: The theory of multiple intelligences*. New York: Basic Books.

Gardner, H. (1991). *The unschooled mind: How children think and how schools should teach*. New York: Basic Books.

Gardner, H. (1993). *Multiple intelligences: The theory in practice*. New York: Basic Books.

Gilman, D., & McDermott, M. (1994). Portfolio collections: An alternative to testing. *Contemporary Education*, 65(2), 73–76.

Haggerty, P. (1992). *Readers' workshop: Real reading*. Richmond Hill, Ontario, Canada: Scholastic Canada.

Heath, S. (1983). *Ways with words: Language, life and work in communities and classrooms*. Cambridge, UK: Cambridge University Press.

Howard, P. (1994). *An owner's manual for the brain*. Austin, TX: Leornian Press.

Joyce, M., & Tallman, J. (1997). *Making the writing and research connection with the I-Search process*. New York: Neal-Schuman Publishers.

Kelly, R. (2000). Working with WebQuests: Making the web accessible to students with disabilities. *Teaching Exceptional Children*, 32(6), 4–13.

Macrorie, K. (1988). *The I-Search paper*. Portsmouth, NH: Boynton/Cook Publishers.

McCarthy, B. (1996). *About learning*. Barrington, IL: Excel.

Means, B., Chelemer, C., & Knapp, M., (Eds.). (1991). *Teaching advanced skills to at-risk learners: Views from research and practice*. San Francisco: Jossey-Bass.

National Research Council. (1990). *How people learn: Brain, mind, experience, and school.* Washington, DC: National Academy Press.

Ornstein, A. (1994, April). Grading practices and policies: An overview and some suggestions. *NASSP Bulletin,* 55–64.

Ornstein, R., & Thompson, R. (1984). *The amazing brain.* Boston: Houghton Mifflin.

Paterson, K. (1981). *The gates of excellence: On reading and writing books for children.* New York: Elsevier/Nelson Books.

Piaget, J. (1969). *The mechanisms of perception.* London: Routledge & Kegan Paul.

Piaget, J. (1978). *Success and understanding.* Cambridge, MA: Harvard University Press.

Reis, S., & Renzulli, J. (1992). Using curriculum compacting to challenge the above average. *Educational Leadership* 50(2), 51–57.

Ross, P. (Ed.). (1993). *National excellence: A case for developing America's talent.* Washington, DC: U.S. Department of Education.

Saracho, O., & Gerstl, C. (1992). Learning differences among at-risk minority students. In B. J. Shade (Ed.), *Culture, style and the educative process* (pp. 105–135). Springfield, IL: Charles C Thomas.

Shade, B. (1989). Creating a culturally compatible classroom. In B. J. Shade (Ed.), *Culture, style and the educative process* (pp. 189–196). Springfield, IL: Charles C Thomas.

Sharan, Y., & Sharan, S. (1992). *Expanding cooperative learning through group investigation.* New York: Teachers College Press.

Sternberg, R. (1985). *Beyond IQ: A triarchic theory of human intelligence.* Cambridge, MA: Cambridge University Press.

Stevenson, C. (1992). *Teaching ten to fourteen year olds.* New York: Longman.

Sullivan, M. (1993). *A meta-analysis of experimental research studies based on the Dunn and Dunn learning styles model and its relationship to academic achievement and performance.* Doctoral dissertation. St. John's University.

Tomlinson, C. (1993). Independent study: A flexible tool for encouraging personal and academic growth in middle school learners. *Middle School Journal,* 25(1), 55–59.

Vygotsky, L. (1962). *Thought and language.* Cambridge, MA: MIT Press.

Wiggins, G., & McTighe, J. (1998). *Understanding by design.* Alexandria, VA: Association for Supervision and Curriculum Development.

Wittrock, M. (Ed.). (1977). *The human brain.* Englewood Cliffs, NJ: Prentice Hall.

For Further Reading

Creating a Community of Learners

Strachota, B. (1996). *On their side: Helping children take charge of their learning.* Greenfield, MA: Northeast Foundation for Children.

A Differentiated Primary Classroom

Maeda, B. (1994). *The multi-age classroom: An inside look at one community of learners.* Cypress, CA: Creating Teaching Press.

Alternative Approaches to Assessment

Herman, J., P. Aschbacher, & Winters, L. (1992). *A practical guide to alternative assessment.* Alexandria, VA: Association for Supervision and Curriculum Development.

Weber, E. (1999). *Student assessments that work: A practical approach.* Boston: Allyn & Bacon.

Graphic Organizers to Meet Needs of Varied Learners

Black, H., & Black, S. (1990). *Organizing thinking: Book one.* Pacific Grove, CA: Critical Thinking Press & Software.

Parks, S., & Black, H. (1992). *Organizing Thinking: Book Two.* Pacific Grove, CA: Critical Thinking Press & Software.

Swartz, R., & Parks, S. (1994). *Infusing the teaching of critical and creative thinking into elementary instruction.* Pacific Grove, CA: Critical Thinking Press & Software.

Reading Support and Development Strategies Across Grades & Content

Billmeyer, R., & Barton, M. (1998). *Teaching reading in the content areas: If not me, then who?* Aurora, CO: Mid-continent Regional Educational Laboratory.

Adapting Instruction to Varied Intelligence Strengths

Armstrong, T. (1994). *Multiple intelligences in the classroom.* Alexandria, VA.: Association for Supervision and Curriculum Development.

Campbell, L., Campbell, C., & Dickinson, D. (1992). *Teaching and learning through multiple intelligences.* Stanwood, WA: New Horizons for Learning.

Curriculum Compacting

Reis, S., & Renzulli, J. (1992). Using curriculum compacting to challenge the above average. *Educational Leadership* 50(2), 51–57.

Starko, A. (1986). *It's about time: Inservice strategies for curriculum compacting.* Mansfield Center, CT: Creative Learning Press.

Adapting Instruction to Varied Learning Styles

American Association of School Administrators. (1991). *Learning styles: Putting research and common sense into practice.* Arlington, VA: Author.

Shade, B. (1989). Creating a culturally compatible classroom. In B. J. Shade, (Ed.), *Culture, style, and the educative process.* Springfield, IL: Charles C Thomas.

Setting Criteria for Tasks and Products

Andrade, H. (2000). Using rubrics to promote thinking and learning. *Educational Leadership, 57*(5),13–18.

Designing and Facilitating Independent Study

Nottage, C., & Morse, V. (2000). *Independent investigation method: A 7-step method for student success in the research process.* Kingston, NH: Active Learning Systems.

Tomlinson, C. (1993). Independent study: A tool for encouraging academic and personal growth. *Middle School Journal* 25(1), 55–59.

Teaching Culturally Diverse Learners

Delpit, L. (1995). *Other people's children: Cultural conflict in the classroom.* New York: The New Press.

Michie, G. (1999). *Holler if you hear me: The education of a teacher and his students.* New York: Teachers College Press.

Rose, M. (1989). *Lives on the boundary.* New York: Penguin.

Suskind, R. (1998). *A hope in the unseen.* New York: Broadway Books.

Differentiating Instruction for Gifted Students

Winebrenner, S. (1992). *Teaching gifted kids in the regular classroom: Strategies every teacher can use to meet the needs of the gifted and talented.* Minneapolis: Free Spirit Publishing.

Differentiating Instruction for Struggling Learners

Winebrenner, S. (1996). *Teaching kids with learning difficulties in the regular classroom.* Minneapolis: Free Spirit Publishing.

Alternatives to Traditional Report Cards

Azwell, T., & Schmar, E. (1995). *Report card on report cards: Alternatives to consider.* Portsmouth, NH: Heinemann.

Wiggins, G. (1996). Honesty and fairness: Toward better grading and reporting. In T. R. Guskey (Ed.), *Communicating student learning* (1996 ASCD Yearbook). Alexandria, VA: Association for Supervision and Curriculum Development.

Index

About the Author

Carol Ann Tomlinson is Associate Professor of Educational Leadership, Foundations and Policy at Curry School of Education, University of Virginia, 287 Ruffner Hall, 405 Emmet Street South, P.O. Box 400277, Charlottesville, VA 22904-4277; telephone: (804) 924-7471; e-mail: cat3y@virginia.edu.

Related ASCD Resources: Differentiated Instruction

ASCD stock numbers are in parentheses.

Audiotapes

2000 ASCD Annual Conference Audiotapes—Top Ten, including "Providing Leadership for Differentiated Classrooms" with Carol Ann Tomlinson (#200098)

"Differentiating Curriculum and Assessment for MixedAbility Classrooms" with Carol Ann Tomlinson (#298309)

"Teaching Gifted Students in Heterogeneous Classes" by Susan Winebrenner (#200177)

"Using Performance Tasks and Rubrics to Support Differentiated Instruction" with Carolyn Callahan, Carol Tomlinson, and Tonya Moon (#297069)

Online Articles

These articles are on the ASCD Web site (http://www.ascd.org) in the Reading Room.

"Differentiating Instruction: Finding Manageable Ways to Meet Individual Needs (Excerpt)" by Scott Willis and Larry Mann, in *Curriculum Update* (Winter 2000)

"How to Differentiate Instruction" in *Classroom Leadership Online* (September 2000)

"Reconcilable Differences?" by Carol Ann Tomlinson, in *Educational Leadership* (September 2000)

"Research Link—Preparing Teachers for Differentiated Instruction" by John H. Holloway, in *Educational Leadership* (September 2000)

Online Courses

These courses are on the ASCD Web site, under Training Opportunities.

The Brain (PD Online Course) (http://www.ascd.org/pdi/pd.html)

Differentiating Instruction (PD Online Course) (http://www.ascd.org/pdi/pd.html)

Online Tutorials, including "Differentiating Instruction" (http://www.ascd.org/frametutorials.html)

Print Products

ASCD Topic Packs—*Differentiated Instruction* (#101032) and *Looping / Multiage Education* (#198217) (both also available online from the ASCD Web site: http://www.ascd.org)

The Differentiated Classroom: Responding to the Needs of All Learners by Carol Ann Tomlinson (#199040)

Educating Everybody's Children: Diverse Teaching Strategies for Diverse Learners edited by Robert W. Cole (#195024)

Leadership for Differentiating Schools and Classrooms by Carol Ann Tomlinson and Susan Demirsky Allan (#100216)

Professional Inquiry Kit

Differentiating Instruction for Mixed Ability Classrooms by Carol Ann Tomlinson, multimedia professional development materials (#196213)

Videotape

Differentiating Instruction with Carol Ann Tomlinson (2-tape set, plus Facilitator's Guide) (#497023)

For more information, visit us on the World Wide Web (http://www.ascd.org), send an e-mail message to member@ascd.org, call the ASCD Service Center (1-800-933-ASCD or 703-578-9600, then press 2), send a fax to 703-575-5400, or write to Information Services, ASCD, 1703 N. Beauregard St., Alexandria, VA 22311-1714 USA.